Frida Kahlo

Frida Kahlo

Hedda Garza

CHELSEA HOUSE PUBLISHERS

NEW YORK ■ PHILADELPHIA

CHELSEA HOUSE PUBLISHERS

Editorial Director: Richard Rennert
Executive Managing Editor: Karyn Gullen Browne
Copy Chief: Robin James
Picture Editor: Adrian G. Allen
Art Director: Robert Mitchell
Manufacturing Director: Gerald Levine
Production Coordinator: Marie Claire Cebrián-Ume

HISPANICS OF ACHIEVEMENT
Senior Editor: Philip Koslow
Staff for FRIDA KAHLO
Copy Editor: Laura Petermann
Designer: M. Cambraia Magalhaes
Picture Researcher: Patricia Burns

7   9   8

Library of Congress Cataloging-in-Publication Data
Garza, Hedda.
Frida Kahlo/Hedda Garza.
p. cm.—(Hispanics of achievement)
Includes bibliographical references and index.
ISBN 0-7910-1698-6
0-7910-1699-4 (pbk.)
1. Kahlo, Frida—Juvenile literature. 2. Painters—Mexico—Biography—Juvenile
literature. [1. Kahlo, Frida. 2. Artists.] I. Title. II. Series.
93-2334
ND259.K33G38 1994
CIP
759.972—dc20
[B]
AC

CONTENTS

HISPANICS OF ACHIEVEMENT

JOAN BAEZ
Mexican-American folksinger

RUBÉN BLADES
Panamanian lawyer and entertainer

JORGE LUIS BORGES
Argentine writer

PABLO CASALS
Spanish cellist and conductor

MIGUEL DE CERVANTES
Spanish writer

CESAR CHAVEZ
Mexican-American labor leader

JULIO CÉSAR CHÁVEZ
Mexican boxing champion

EL CID
Spanish military leader

HENRY CISNEROS
Mexican-American political leader

ROBERTO CLEMENTE
Puerto Rican baseball player

SALVADOR DALÍ
Spanish painter

PLÁCIDO DOMINGO
Spanish singer

GLORIA ESTEFAN
Cuban-American singer

GABRIEL GARCÍA MÁRQUEZ
Colombian writer

FRANCISCO JOSÉ DE GOYA
Spanish painter

JULIO IGLESIAS
Spanish singer

RAUL JULIA
Puerto Rican actor

FRIDA KAHLO
Mexican painter

JOSÉ MARTÍ
Cuban revolutionary and poet

RITA MORENO
Puerto Rican singer and actress

PABLO NERUDA
Chilean poet and diplomat

OCTAVIO PAZ
Mexican poet and critic

PABLO PICASSO
Spanish artist

ANTHONY QUINN
Mexican-American actor

DIEGO RIVERA
Mexican painter

LINDA RONSTADT
Mexican-American singer

ANTONIO LÓPEZ DE SANTA ANNA
Mexican general and politician

GEORGE SANTAYANA
Spanish philosopher and poet

JUNÍPERO SERRA
Spanish missionary and explorer

LEE TREVINO
Mexican-American golfer

PANCHO VILLA
Mexican revolutionary

CHELSEA HOUSE PUBLISHERS

HISPANICS OF ACHIEVEMENT

Rodolfo Cardona

The Spanish language and many other elements of Spanish culture are present in the United States today and have been since the country's earliest beginnings. Some of these elements have come directly from the Iberian Peninsula; others have come indirectly, by way of Mexico, the Caribbean basin, and the countries of Central and South America.

Spanish culture has influenced America in many subtle ways, and consequently many Americans remain relatively unaware of the extent of its impact. The vast majority of them recognize the influence of Spanish culture in America, but they often do not realize the great importance and long history of that influence. This is partly because Americans have tended to judge the Hispanic influence in the United States in statistical terms rather than to look closely at the ways in which individual Hispanics have profoundly affected American culture. For this reason, it is fitting that Americans obtain more than a passing acquaintance with the origins of these Spanish cultural elements and gain an understanding of how they have been woven into the fabric of American society.

It is well documented that Spanish seafarers were the first to explore and colonize many of the early territories of what is today called the United States of America. For this reason, students of geography discover Hispanic names all over the map of the United States. For instance, the Strait of Juan de Fuca was named after the Spanish explorer who first navigated the waters of the Pacific Northwest; the names of states such as Arizona (arid zone), Montana (mountain), Florida (thus named because it was reached on Easter Sunday, which in Spanish is called the feast of Pascua Florida), and California (named after a fictitious land in one of the first and probably the most popular among the Spanish novels of chivalry, *Amadis of Gaul*) are all derived from Spanish; and there are numerous mountains, rivers, canyons, towns, and cities with Spanish names throughout the United States.

Not only explorers but many other illustrious figures in Spanish history have helped define American culture. For example, the 13th-century king of Spain, Alfonso X, also known as the Learned, may be unknown to the majority of Americans, but his work on the codification of Spanish law has greatly influenced the evolution of American law, particularly in the jurisdictions of the Southwest. For this contribution a statue of him stands in the rotunda of the Capitol in Washington, D.C. Likewise, the name Diego Rivera may be unfamiliar to most Americans, but this Mexican painter influenced many American artists whose paintings, commissioned during the Great Depression and the New Deal era of the 1930s, adorn the walls of government buildings throughout the United States. In recent years the contributions of Puerto Ricans, Mexicans, Mexican Americans (Chicanos), and Cubans in American cities such as Boston, Chicago, Los Angeles, Miami, Minneapolis, New York, and San Antonio have been enormous.

The importance of the Spanish language in this vast cultural complex cannot be overstated. Spanish, after all, is second only to English as the most widely spoken of Western languages within the United States as well as in the entire world. The popularity of the Spanish language in America has a long history.

In addition to Spanish exploration of the New World, the great Spanish literary tradition served as a vehicle for bringing the language and culture to America. Interest in Spanish literature in America began when English immigrants brought with them translations of Spanish masterpieces of the Golden Age. As early as 1683, private libraries in Philadelphia and Boston contained copies of the first picaresque novel, *Lazarillo de Tormes*, translations of Francisco de Quevedo's *Los Sueños*, and copies of the immortal epic of reality and illusion *Don Quixote*, by the great Spanish writer Miguel de Cervantes. It would not be surprising if Cotton Mather, the arch-Puritan, read *Don Quixote* in its original Spanish, if only to enrich his vocabulary in preparation for his writing *La fe del cristiano en 24 artículos de la Institución de Cristo, enviada a los españoles para que abran sus ojos* (The Christian's Faith in 24 Articles of the Institution of Christ, Sent to the Spaniards to Open Their Eyes), published in Boston in 1699.

Over the years, Spanish authors and their works have had a vast influence on American literature—from Washington Irving, John Steinbeck, and Ernest Hemingway in the novel to Henry Wadsworth Longfellow and Archibald MacLeish in poetry. Such important American writers as James Fenimore Cooper, Edgar Allan Poe, Walt Whitman, Mark Twain, and Herman Melville all owe a sizable debt to the Spanish literary tradition. Some writers, such as Willa Cather and Maxwell Anderson, who explored Spanish themes they came into contact with in the American Southwest and Mexico, were influenced less directly but no less profoundly.

Important contributions to a knowledge of Spanish culture in the United States were also made by many lesser known individuals—teachers, publishers, historians, entrepreneurs, and others—with a love for Spanish culture. One of the most significant of these contributions was made by Abiel Smith, a Harvard College graduate of the class of 1764, when he bequeathed stock worth $20,000 to Harvard for the support of a professor of French and Spanish. By 1819 this endowment had produced enough income to appoint a professor, and the philologist and humanist George Ticknor became the first holder of the Abiel

Smith Chair, which was the very first endowed Chair at Harvard University. Other illustrious holders of the Smith Chair would include the poets Henry Wadsworth Longfellow and James Russell Lowell.

A highly respected teacher and scholar, Ticknor was also a collector of Spanish books, and as such he made a very special contribution to America's knowledge of Spanish culture. He was instrumental in amassing for Harvard libraries one of the first and most impressive collections of Spanish books in the United States. He also had a valuable personal collection of Spanish books and manuscripts, which he bequeathed to the Boston Public Library.

With the creation of the Abiel Smith Chair, Spanish language and literature courses became part of the curriculum at Harvard, which also went on to become the first American university to offer graduate studies in Romance languages. Other colleges and universities throughout the United States gradually followed Harvard's example, and today Spanish language and culture may be studied at most American institutions of higher learning.

No discussion of the Spanish influence in the United States, however brief, would be complete without a mention of the Spanish influence on art. Important American artists such as John Singer Sargent, James A. M. Whistler, Thomas Eakins, and Mary Cassatt all explored Spanish subjects and experimented with Spanish techniques. Virtually every serious American artist living today has studied the work of the Spanish masters as well as the great 20th-century Spanish painters Salvador Dalí, Joan Miró, and Pablo Picasso.

The most pervasive Spanish influence in America, however, has probably been in music. Compositions such as Leonard Bernstein's *West Side Story*, the Latinization of William Shakespeare's *Romeo and Juliet* set in New York's Puerto Rican quarter, and Aaron Copland's *Salon Mexico* are two obvious examples. In general, one can hear the influence of Latin rhythms—from tango to mambo, from guaracha to salsa—in virtually every form of American music.

This series of biographies, which Chelsea House has published under the general title HISPANICS OF ACHIEVEMENT, constitutes further recognition of—and a renewed effort to bring forth to the consciousness of America's young people—the contributions that Hispanic people have made not only in the United States but throughout the civilized world. The men and women who are featured in this series have attained a high level of accomplishment in their respective fields of endeavor and have made a permanent mark on American society.

The title of this series must be understood in its broadest possible sense: The term *Hispanics* is intended to include Spaniards, Spanish Americans, and individuals from many countries whose language and culture have either direct or indirect Spanish origins. The names of many of the people included in this series will be immediately familiar; others will be less recognizable. All, however, have attained recognition within their own countries, and often their fame has transcended their borders.

The series HISPANICS OF ACHIEVEMENT thus addresses the attainments and struggles of Hispanic people in the United States and seeks to tell the stories of individuals whose personal and professional lives in some way reflect the larger Hispanic experience. These stories are exemplary of what human beings can accomplish, often against daunting odds and by extraordinary personal sacrifice, where there is conviction and determination. Fray Junípero Serra, the 18th-century Spanish Franciscan missionary, is one such individual. Although in very poor health, he devoted the last 15 years of his life to the foundation of missions throughout California—then a mostly unsettled expanse of land—in an effort to bring a better life to Native Americans through the cultivation of crafts and animal husbandry. An example from recent times, the Mexican-American labor leader Cesar Chavez battled bitter opposition and made untold personal sacrifices in his effort to help poor agricultural workers who have been exploited for decades on farms throughout the Southwest.

The talent with which each one of these men and women may have been endowed required dedication and hard work to develop and become fully realized. Many of them have enjoyed rewards for their efforts during their own lifetime, whereas others have died poor and unrecognized. For some it took a long time to achieve their goals, for others success came at an early age, and for still others the struggle continues. All of them, however, stand out as people whose lives have made a difference, whose achievements we need to recognize today and should continue to honor in the future.

Frida Kahlo

THE BUS TO HELL

Frida Kahlo at the age of 19. Throughout her high school years, Kahlo dreamed of becoming a doctor, but shortly after her 18th birthday, a serious accident put an end to that ambition. Pursuing a new destiny, she began an artistic career that eventually brought her world fame.

Late in the drizzly afternoon of September 17, 1925, Frida Kahlo and Alejandro Gómez Arias raced to catch a bus that would take them to the suburb of Coyoacán, an hour's travel from the center of Mexico City, where they had been browsing at a street fair. Kahlo, 18 years old, was an exotic sight as her thick black hair flew in the wind. Her sparkling dark eyes were set off by luxuriant eyebrows that nearly met. Her sweetheart, called Alex by his friends, was a strikingly handsome young man.

People turned to stare at the unusual couple, but they focused mostly on Kahlo. Dressed in workman's overalls, she was a shocking spectacle in conservative, Catholic Mexico. Several people made nasty comments about her tomboyish appearance, speaking loudly enough for her to hear them.

As usual, Kahlo was talking a mile a minute. After graduation, she told Gómez, she would attend medical school and become a famous doctor, *if* she found a way to get the money. On the other hand, perhaps they should run off to San Francisco together, escape from the church-dominated atmosphere of Mexico City, and live where life was freer for a year or two. A skeptical Gómez asked: if Frida had no money for medical school, how did she plan to live in San Francisco?

Kahlo laughed at her boyfriend's practical streak, but her gaiety masked a deep concern about his feelings for her. It was not only her ever-present insecurity about her right leg, which was thinner and weaker than its mate from her bout with polio when she was six. Her "pegleg," as some of her classmates had bluntly named it, could be hidden under pants or long skirts. She could also divert attention from it with laughter, charm, and intellectual conversation. But as she glanced at Gómez, Kahlo wondered whether he still loved her.

Since he had begun attending the university, Gómez seemed to have less and less time for Kahlo. During the summer, Kahlo had completed a typing course at a business school and worked at several boring jobs in Mexico City. The money had helped her family, but her main motivation for seeking employment had been to remove herself from her mother's watchful eye and to be free to arrange secret trysts with her lover. Yet most of the time he had been too busy to meet her. She suspected that Gómez's ardor had cooled because of the scandals about her activities over the summer. She worried that he might never trust her again.

A bus appeared at the end of the street, so brightly colored that it resembled a circus car. As the gaudy vehicle headed for the bus stop, a waiting group waved excitedly. Recently introduced in Mexico City, the buses were still a welcome novelty, although they were not as safe as the now nearly empty trolleys. The drivers were young and arrogant, *muy macho*—which in Mexico meant that they felt brave and invincible, thinking that the Virgin of Guadalupe medals hanging above the driver's seat would protect them from all harm. There had already been several accidents. But the young students felt invincible too. The future seemed especially bright for Kahlo, one of the few women permitted to enroll in Mexico's most prestigious high school, El Preparatorio—the National Preparatory School.

As the bus came to a squealing stop, Kahlo and Gómez clambered aboard and made their way past the crowded benches lining both sides to two seats near the back. The bus lurched ahead past the colorful San Juan market, its stalls filled with flowers, fruits, vegetables, and Mexican handicrafts displayed to catch the eyes of tourists. At a nearby intersection, a two-car electric trolley was rumbling ponderously along the tracks.

Each driver made up his mind to brazen out the crossing, an almost daily game. Usually a collision was avoided by a hairbreadth. This time the game ended in tragedy.

Before the bus could clear the tracks, the trolley plowed straight into it. Within seconds the area was a

While recovering in 1926, Kahlo made this sketch of the accident that had nearly taken her life. The memory was so painful, however, that she could not create a detailed picture of the scene until many years later.

scene of horror. The bus was shoved along by the much heavier trolley until it careened into the wall of a building and splintered into pieces. Bodies flew into the air, some of them landing on the tracks, where they were cruelly crushed beneath the wheels of the trolley's second car.

Gómez, badly cut and bruised, managed to climb from under the trolley. Dazedly, he searched for Kahlo and found her lying near the tracks. The force of the crash had torn away most of her clothing. Her body was covered with blood and with a glittering gold powder that had been spilled by an artist or housepainter who had also been a passenger on the hellish bus. From the sidewalk a child's voice called out, "The ballerina! Help the ballerina!" To the child, Kahlo resembled a dancer garbed in a golden leotard.

Gómez, numb with horror, saw that Kahlo's slender body had been pierced by a metal rod. A section of a handrail from the bus had gored her deeply, but by some miracle, she was still alive. Her eyes were open. Deeply in shock, she did not seem to feel any pain or to realize how seriously she was injured.

A workman in overalls approached, put an arm around Gómez, and bent down to examine Kahlo. Deciding that the metal rod had to be removed, he braced himself by placing a knee on the injured woman's body and then tugged with all his strength. As the rod was yanked out, Kahlo's scream of agony pierced the air, drowning out the sound of approaching sirens. Lifting Kahlo gently, Gómez carried her across the street to a billiard parlor, placed her on a pool table, and covered her with his tattered coat. An ambulance arrived and took them to the nearest hospital.

Following the triage system of leaving hopeless patients for last, the doctors, believing that there was no chance for Kahlo, turned their attention to the less seriously injured victims. Gómez pleaded with them

los Eposor guillermo Kahlo y Matilde c. de Kahlo Dan lar gracias-
a la Virgen de los Dolores por haber Salvado-

This retablo, *or votive offering, was Kahlo's first and only painting of the 1925 bus accident. The figure at the upper left is the Virgin of Sorrows, and the writing at the bottom expresses the Kahlos' gratitude to the Virgin for sparing the life of their daughter.*

not to give up, and finally Kahlo was rushed into emergency surgery. As the surgical team examined the young woman's broken body and saw the blood still spurting from the gaping wound in her abdomen, none of them believed that she could live through the night.

They were mistaken. The slender young tomboy was deceptively tough. She had survived her childhood bout with polio, and she survived the terrible injuries inflicted on her by the harrowing bus crash. Though tormented by endless medical problems and excruciating pain, she went on to live a rich and tumultuous life for another 30 years, in the course of which she became one of the 20th century's most original and memorable artists.

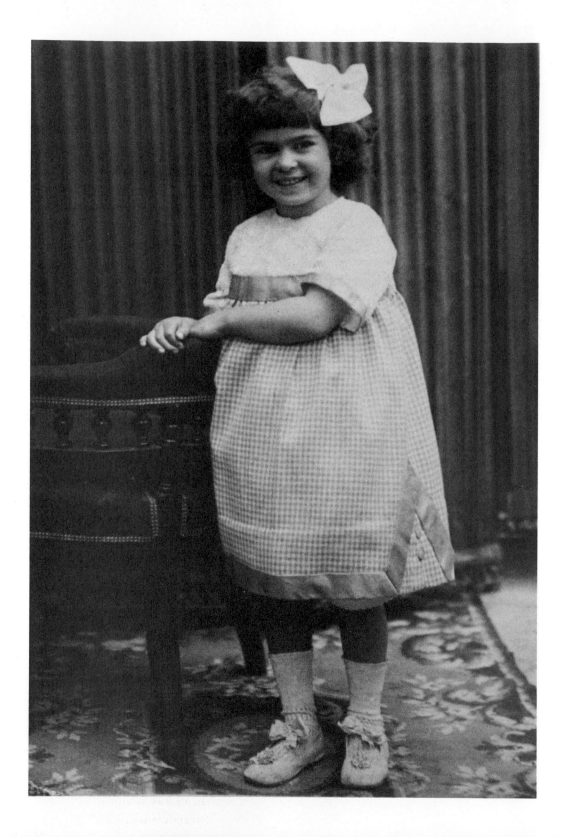

THE CACHUCHAS

Frida Kahlo, photographed at the age of three. Strictly raised by her mother, Frida emerged as a rebellious teenager, discarding her frilly dresses for workman's overalls and living life according to her own rules.

Frida Kahlo was born at 8:30 on the rainy morning of July 6, 1907, in the same stucco house in Coyoacán that later became the Frida Kahlo Museum. She was baptized Magdalena Carmen Frieda Kahlo y Calderón, but to her parents, Guillermo Kahlo and Matilde Calderón Kahlo, as well as her five sisters, she was always simply Frida.

Guillermo Kahlo's own parents, Jacob Heinrich Kahl and Henrietta Kaufmann Kahl, were Hungarian Jews. Like many Jews in 19th-century Europe, they were always looking for a safe haven from pogroms— raids on their neighborhoods by soldiers and civilians who burned their homes and looted their belongings. They were also subjected to laws restricting their rights to jobs, housing, and education. When Germany granted full civil rights to Jews in 1870, the Kahls migrated to Germany and settled in Baden-Baden, where Jacob Kahl opened a successful jewelry and photographic supply business. Their son Wilhelm was born in 1872.

Wilhelm was a scholarly boy, and when he finished high school his prosperous father was able to send him to the prestigious University of Nuremberg. Unfortunately, his bright prospects were cut off quickly. After suffering a head injury during a fall in 1890, Wilhelm developed severe epilepsy. For the rest of his life he was subject to almost daily convulsions. That same year, his mother died, and his father married a woman whom Wilhelm disliked. In 1891, eager to make a fresh start elsewhere, 19-year-old Wilhelm Kahl left Germany.

Mexico was a logical destination for Kahl. After decades of political turmoil and foreign invasions, General Porfirio Díaz had seized the nation's presidency in 1876. Determined to industrialize his country, he invited European businessmen and professionals to make Mexico their new homeland. To keep wages low and make land available to the newcomers, Díaz launched a reign of terror, breaking workers' strikes and creating the *rurales*, a special police force charged with enforcing his plan to give away the land of poor peasants to wealthy landowners. As the suffering of the poor deepened, Mexico's minuscule middle class began expanding.

Even in this climate, Wilhelm Kahl had difficulty establishing himself. Although he changed his name to the more Spanish-sounding Guillermo Kahlo, he could not change his blue eyes or his heavy German accent. Shortly after he arrived, the recession of 1892 began, and the promised opportunities no longer existed. Connecting with other German immigrants, Kahlo took a succession of odd jobs. He worked as a cashier in a glassware store, a book salesman, and a clerk in a jewelry store. In 1894, he married a Mexican woman of Indian ancestry. She bore him two daughters, María Luisa and Margarita, but died in 1898, during the second childbirth. Kahlo was alone again, only this time with two baby daughters to raise.

Matilde Calderón y González, his co-worker at the jewelry store, had sympathy for Kahlo and tried to comfort him. Before long, she agreed to become his second wife. She did not, however, crave the role of stepmother: as soon as they were old enough, María

Luisa and Margarita were bundled off to a convent school. Their visits home were few and far between. Matilde gave birth to four children, all of them girls—Matilde (known as Matita), Adriana, Frida, and Cristina. Of the four, Matilde favored her firstborn; Guillermo clearly loved Frida the best, considering her the most intelligent.

Kahlo's prospects improved considerably when his new father-in-law, Antonio Calderón, who was a photographer, lent him a camera and took him on a photographic tour of Mexico to record the old colonial and Indian architectural wonders. Impressed with the photographs, the Díaz government commissioned the two men to illustrate a series of books planned for the 1910 centennial celebration of Mexico's independence from Spain. By 1904, three years before Frida's birth, Kahlo was able to buy some land in a fashionable neighborhood in Coyoacán. He built a spacious one-story house, graced with many large windows, overlooking a large patio and a tree-shaded

Guillermo and Matilde Calderón Kahlo, photographed on their wedding day in 1898. The third of the couple's four daughters, Frida Kahlo was often in conflict with her mother but enjoyed a warm and affectionate relationship with her father, who doted on her after she was stricken with poliomyelitis.

garden. The outer walls were painted a striking shade of cobalt, and the structure quickly became known as the Blue House. The Kahlo children spent many happy hours romping among the trees, plants, and pottery of their backyard greenery.

But the family's good fortune was quickly disrupted by popular revolt against the Díaz regime. In 1910, the Mexican Revolution had its true beginning when Francisco Indalécio Madero campaigned for the presidency on a program of democratic reforms. When the government threw Madero into prison, soldiers of the Mexican Liberal party (PLM), the peasant armies of Emiliano Zapata, and a pro-Madero group led by Francisco "Pancho" Villa went into action. In May 1911, these forces defeated Díaz's *federales,* and the dictator fled. Later that year, Madero was elected president amid celebration and optimism, and Zapata ordered his men to lay down their arms. Years later, Frida Kahlo would give her birthdate as 1910, the official beginning of the revolution, preferring it to the less significant date of 1907.

As Mexicans celebrated their new beginning, Guillermo Kahlo, with his sponsorship gone, saw his affluence abruptly end. Despite his reputation, photographic commissions were few and far between. Matilde Kahlo scrimped and saved, an effort little appreciated by her daughter Frida. Later, Frida Kahlo claimed that her mother was illiterate but that "she knew how to count money!" In fact, Matilde Kahlo had been well educated in her convent school, and her good economic management probably saved the family home.

The Kahlos mortgaged the Blue House, took in boarders, and sold off much of their luxurious French furniture. Matilde Kahlo's health deteriorated. She suffered dizzy spells not unlike her husband's and often stayed in bed, while her two eldest daughters,

Matita and Adriana, cared for the little ones, Frida and
Cristina.

In 1913, when Frida was only six years old, she fell
victim to poliomyelitis, also known as infantile paraly-
sis, a dreaded childhood disease. (Until Jonas Salk
developed a vaccine in the 1950s, thousands of children were killed or crippled each year by the polio
virus.) For months, Frida endured terrible pains in
her right leg. When she recovered, her right leg was
shorter and thinner than the left, and she walked with
a pronounced limp. The child who had once been a
joyous tomboy became thin, sad, and withdrawn.

Faced with his favorite daughter's affliction,
Guillermo Kahlo sprang into action. He had seldom
paid much attention to his family, coming home from
his studio each night to eat a solitary meal and retire
to his study, where he read German classics and played
German music on the piano. He was a withdrawn
man with few friends. But now Frida became the
center of his attention. The doctors said that exercise
might strengthen the muscles of Frida's right leg, so
her father took her to a nearby park and encouraged
her to run and climb. On frequent nature walks, they
collected leaves, insects, and stones, bringing them
home to examine them under a microscope and draw
them. Guillermo allowed Frida to use his paints and
taught her to draw meticulously. Frida's leg gradually
grew stronger and her limp almost vanished, but for
the rest of her life, she would wear clothes that hid her
withered limb.

Frida and her father grew very close. She was even
able to tease him, calling him "Herr Kahlo" for his stiff
Germanic personality, formal dress, and heavy accent.
Later, she often accompanied him on his photographic expeditions through Mexico City, helping
him if he was suddenly stricken by an epileptic attack
and guarding his camera until he recovered.

In later life, Frida Kahlo would tell interviewers that her childhood had been "marvelous," and she attributed that happiness to her father. On the other hand, Frida always resented her mother. Matilde Kahlo was a strictly religious Catholic and raised her daughters accordingly. When they were small, she took them every day to the nearby Church of St. John the Baptist, where they would squirm and yawn during endless hours of ritual. Before every meal, the girls were required to say prayers. Margarita eventually became a nun, but Frida and Cristina detested religion. At home Matilde Kahlo taught her daughters to sew, embroider, cook, and clean, hoping they would be prepared for any hard times that might befall them. Frida chafed under her mother's strict regime, longing for freedom. She secretly named her mother "mi Jefe" (my chief).

When Frida discovered her mother drowning a litter of baby rats in the basement one day, she never

The Kahlo family (Frida is seated on the left) poses on the porch of the Blue House, around 1911. The house is now the property of the Mexican people: as the Frida Kahlo Museum, it endures as a tribute to a great artist's life and work.

forgave her for what she regarded as an act of cruelty. Her reaction may have been a response to Matilde's treatment of Frida's big sister Matita.

When Frida was seven, 15-year-old Matita eloped with her boyfriend. Frida covered up the signs of her escape and made excuses for her sister's absence until she was safely far away. When she learned the truth, Matilde refused to allow Matita to visit the house, despite the pleading of her sisters.

Even with his reduced financial circumstances, Guillermo Kahlo would not give up on his plans for Frida's future. In 1922, when she was 15, Frida took the entrance examinations for the prestigious National Preparatory School. The brightest young men in Mexico were studying there, and recently the school had become coeducational. When Frida was accepted, she became one of only 35 young women in a student body of 2,000.

In the fall of 1922, as Frida Kahlo left her quiet Coyoacán neighborhood to begin the hour-long trolley trip to Mexico City for her first day at the National Preparatory, her mother watched her anxiously. The very idea of coeducation upset Matilde Kahlo, and here was her young daughter traveling to a high school filled with young men in the heart of sinful and dangerous Mexico City.

True, Frida looked like a proper German Catholic schoolgirl, with her neatly braided hair, dark skirt, white middy blouse, tie, boots, and straw hat. But the young girl had already displayed signs of her rebellious nature.

Glad to be away from the watchful eye of her mother, Frida felt her heart racing as the trolley took her to a new and exciting world. In those days, the patio-encircled, red-brick building that housed the National Preparatory was located close to the University of Mexico. The area teemed with students and featured shops of every description, movie houses, and peddlers hawking their wares. Colorfully dressed street musicians, known as mariachis, serenaded the crowds of pedestrians.

Mexico City had changed enormously while Frida was attending grade school in the suburbs. The nation as a whole was emerging from more than a decade of revolutionary turbulence in which 2 million people had been killed or wounded. Several popular revolutionary leaders had fallen before assassins' bullets—Madero, Zapata, and, just two years earlier, President Venustiano Carranza. Alvaro Obregón, elected president in 1920, attempted to carry out the Mexican Revolution's radical 1917 Constitution. His new minister of education, José Vasconcelos, embarked on an educational campaign to wipe out illiteracy in Mexico, equipping libraries, training teachers, and opening many schools to women.

Frida found herself surrounded by the future intellectuals of Mexico, most of them far more sophisticated than she. They had organized themselves into various cliques, according to their interests. There were groups of political activists, artists, sports enthusiasts, debaters, book lovers, and religious and antireligious thinkers. The Cachuchas, whose name derived from the knitted red caps they wore, were the group that Frida found most attractive. Although they were among the best students in the school, they were famous for their tricks and pranks and their total lack of respect for rules. Most of the other students considered them immoral troublemakers. The Cachuchas consisted of seven boys and one girl, and their leader was Alejandro Gómez Arias.

Frida changed her appearance radically in order to fit in with the Cachuchas. She cut her hair in straight bangs and began wearing overalls, shocking her mother and her neighbors in Coyoacán. After she joined the rebellious group, she became famous for outdoing the boys in the use of foul language and the art of pulling pranks.

When they were not in class, the 35 National Preparatory girls were instructed to congregate in a special area on the top floor of the school's largest patio. But Frida seldom obeyed that rule. She preferred to hang out with the boys at the Ibero-American Library, a few blocks from the school. She considered most of the other girls silly gossips. Her only girlfriends were two other tomboys, Adelina Zendejas and the other female member of the Cachuchas, Carmen Jaime. Both women would remain Kahlo's friends for life. Jaime, a brilliant student of philosophy, dressed in masculine clothing and went by the nicknames of James and Vampire (because of a black cape she often wore).

In a short time, Frida became the leading mischief maker of the Cachuchas, playing tricks on teachers and cutting classes that bored her. Nevertheless, she did well at her studies because she was gifted with an excellent memory.

As part of Vasconcelos's cultural program, he invited Mexican artists to paint gigantic murals on the walls of public buildings to glorify Mexican history. In 1921, Diego Rivera, the most famous artist in Mexico, arrived at the National Preparatory to help decorate the walls of the auditorium. The students were ordered to stay away from the work area, strengthening the desire of the Cachuchas to do just the opposite.

The 36-year-old Rivera, tall and obese, dressed in baggy pants and a huge Stetson hat instead of the black suit and dress shirt customary among Mexican men. He talked loudly as he perched high on the scaffolding. Making him an even more interesting target for the Cachuchas, Rivera had a reputation as a tireless skirt-chaser. He had left a wife and child behind in Paris and was married to his principal model, Lupe Marín, but an endless parade of other beautiful models were always by his side. With Frida often in the lead, the Cachuchas set about tormenting Rivera: soaping the stairs in the hope that he would tumble down them, bursting water balloons over the painters' heads, stealing their lunches, and even setting fire to the wood shavings on the floor, filling the room with smoke. Rivera took to wearing a pistol in his belt to scare off the troublesome students.

Frida particularly enjoyed hiding in the doorway and taunting the beleaguered artist. When Rivera flirted with a model, she would call out, "Watch out Diego, Lupe is coming!" She jokingly bragged to one of the other girls that she would someday have Rivera's baby. Later, this comment gave rise to a myth about Kahlo's early love for Rivera.

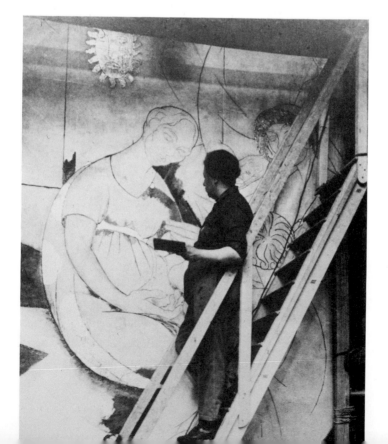

Diego Rivera at work on a mural at the National Preparatory School in 1922. Tormented incessantly by the Cachuchas, a mischievous band of students of whom Kahlo was the ringleader, Rivera took to wearing a pistol in his belt while he was at work.

Actually, Frida had fallen in love with Alejandro Gómez Arias, and by 1923 they had become lovers. Matilde Kahlo insisted that her daughter come straight home from school and kept a close watch on her activities. In order to evade her mother's scrutiny, Frida offered to help her father in his photography studio after school—in reality, she slipped out to meet Gómez. For a while he was her only boyfriend, but Kahlo seemed to need love and attention desperately. Perhaps her "pegleg" continued to make her insecure, or perhaps her strict upbringing made rebellion even more of a challenge. Whatever the reason, by the summer of 1925, she was no longer faithful to Gómez.

During that summer, Kahlo took several jobs but lost them all. As a cashier in a pharmacy, she could not keep the receipts straight. Working in a factory and a lumberyard, she hated the boring routine. All the while she worked on her secretarial skills, trying to land a spot at the Ministry of Education library, where the pay was higher and she could surround herself with books all day. During that period, a female supervisor who interviewed Frida also became her lover.

Before the summer was over, Frida's father helped her land an apprenticeship with his printer friend Fernando Fernández. Frida began to show talent as an artist, learning to copy prints for engraving. She also had an affair with her boss.

Sexual activity outside of marriage was the cause for much gossip in those decades, and Frida was a favorite subject for wagging tongues. It did not take long for the scandals to reach Alejandro Gómez's ears. Frida did not want to lose her sweetheart, but despite his anger and jealousy, she refused to promise to be faithful.

With this issue rankling between them, the young lovers rushed to the doomed bus on September 17.

THE BIRTH
OF AN ARTIST

O n September 17, 1925, after hours of emergency
surgery in the Red Cross Hospital, Frida Kahlo
was carried into a gloomy ward, the place where
people without much money were taken. Twenty-four
other seriously ill and injured patients occupied the
beds surrounding hers. One overworked nurse tended
to all of them.

Kahlo awakened to find herself encased in a cof-
finlike plaster cast with only her head exposed. In
addition to the terrible wound in her abdomen, her
spine had been fractured in three places; she had also
suffered a fractured pelvis, a dislocated shoulder, two
broken ribs, and shattered bones in her right leg and
foot. She was in almost unbearable pain, an agony that
would persist for most of the rest of her life. In
terrifying nightmares, she relived the accident and
heard the screams of the other victims.

Her parents did not come to visit her for almost
three weeks. When he heard of the crash, Guillermo
Kahlo's health took a turn for the worse. Matilde
Kahlo wept constantly and would not speak for days.
The long trip to Mexico City was too much for them.
Frida's banished sister, Matita, read about the accident

Frida Kahlo (standing at left, in man's suit) in a 1926 photograph with members of her family, including her mother (middle row, center) and her sister Cristina (front row). The Kahlo family, beset by financial pressures, illness, and emotional conflicts, was described by Frida as "one of the saddest I have ever seen."

in the newspapers and spent hours each day at the hospital, helping the nurse and cheering up the patients. Although some of the Cachuchas visited, Alex Gómez was not among them, even after his own injuries had healed.

As soon as Kahlo could move one of her arms, she wrote to Gómez, describing the horrors of her injuries and treatments. "It harmed everybody, and me most of all," she wrote, despite the fact that several people had died during and after the bus crash. She begged him to visit, telling him, "Now I see how much I love you with all my soul." Still he did not come.

On October 17, 1925, exactly one month after the accident, Matilde Kahlo took her daughter home. There, Frida's situation worsened. Still confined to her bed, the high-spirited young woman, who had learned to leap and run after her bout with polio, remained immobilized with splints and plaster casts, suffering terribly. She became self-centered and obsessed with the thought that she was about to die.

Alejandro Gómez Arias, photographed around 1929, when he had achieved prominence as a student leader. After the bus accident, Kahlo decided that Gómez was the man she truly loved, but he showed little interest in continuing the relationship.

Most of Kahlo's school friends lived in Mexico City, and they visited infrequently. Kahlo believed that her family's eccentricities discouraged them from coming. Matita continued to visit, but Matilde Kahlo, fixed in a black mood, still would have nothing to do with her eldest daughter. She stormed out whenever Matita entered the house. Guillermo Kahlo withdrew into himself, depressed over Frida's condition and the mountain of hospital bills. In letters to Gómez, Kahlo described her family as "one of the saddest I have ever seen."

What disturbed Kahlo most, however, was her sweetheart's continued absence. Appealing to Gómez's sense of pity, Kahlo's letters were filled with detailed descriptions of her physical suffering. She wrote about her fears that she would never walk again and drew sketches of her own weeping face. But when other visitors came, Kahlo clowned and laughed as though nothing had changed.

Gómez finally wrote back and tried to visit on at least one occasion, but he did not get into the house. Matilde Kahlo had a fainting spell when she saw him, and Cristina Kahlo ran into the street to stop Gómez from coming up to the front door, telling him the absurd story that her bedridden sister was not at home.

Despite her pessimism, Kahlo's love of life prevailed. Her broken bones healed, and her spirits improved when she was able to leave her bed and walk. Still in pain and limping, Kahlo decided not to return to school. "I felt I had energies for anything except studying to become a doctor," she wrote in one of her many notes to Gómez.

On December 18, three months after the accident, Kahlo amazed everyone by traveling to Mexico City to try to see Alejandro Gómez in person. She went to his home in the morning and waited in vain for hours, then returned later in the day. Again she was told that he was not at home. She looked up another school chum and learned that Gómez had gossiped about her behavior. "The fact is now no one wants to be my friend because I have lost my reputation," she wrote him bitterly. "I will never forget that you, whom I loved as I loved myself or more, saw me as a Nahui [one of Diego Rivera's models, considered promiscuous by the Preparatoria students]. Every time you tell me that you don't want to talk to me anymore, you've done it as if you wanted to take a weight off yourself. I am being driven crazy."

Kahlo made several more taxing journeys to Mexico City, telling Gómez where she would be and waiting in vain for him to arrive. The exertion placed too much strain on her weakened spine, and in the summer of 1926, Kahlo had a serious relapse. Once more she was confined to her bed, immobilized with casts and corsets. A constraining apparatus encasing her right foot was added.

Lonely, immobile, and in pain, Kahlo begged her father to allow her to use his paints. Matilde Kahlo ordered a special easel for her bedridden young daughter, and a mirror was installed on the inside of the canopy over her bed.

Aside from the caricatures she had scribbled in school and the drawings for Fernando Fernández, Kahlo had never paid much attention to art. She began teaching herself from art books, studying the works of the Italian Renaissance artists and experimenting with the colors in her father's paint box. She painted portraits of visitors and relatives who were willing to sit and pose for her and gave the paintings away as gifts.

Then she turned to the mirror on her canopy and painted the first of many self-portraits, a gift for Alex Gómez, who was still avoiding her. She completed the portrait in time for the first anniversary of the bus accident. It portrayed her in perfect health and wear-

La Adelita, Pancho Villa, and Frida, *painted by Kahlo in 1927, included one of her earliest self-portraits. Bedridden after her 1925 accident, Kahlo began to experiment with her father's paints; though she had never studied art, early works such as this one showed her budding talent.*

ing an elegant red velvet dress. Her hand was held out, like a symbol of entreaty, begging her lover to return. "Put it in a low place so that you can see it as if you are looking at me," she wrote in her note accompanying the portrait.

The friendship between Kahlo and Gómez resumed, but their romance was apparently dead. In March 1927, Gómez, now studying law, left for a work-study program in Germany, telling Kahlo he would return in July. As he was about to depart, he claimed falsely that an aunt was having surgery and he had to rush off to help her, avoiding a personal farewell at Kahlo's bedside.

When Gómez returned in November 1927, he found Kahlo up and about, busy painting again. He resumed his studies at the university and became a student political leader. As Gómez and the rest of her friends became deeply involved in political activities, Kahlo frequently journeyed to Mexico City to join them at their rallies and meetings. She was always charming and witty in public, and her friends, except for Gómez, were unaware of her suffering.

At this time, Mexico's political life was once again in turmoil. Six months after his re-election in January

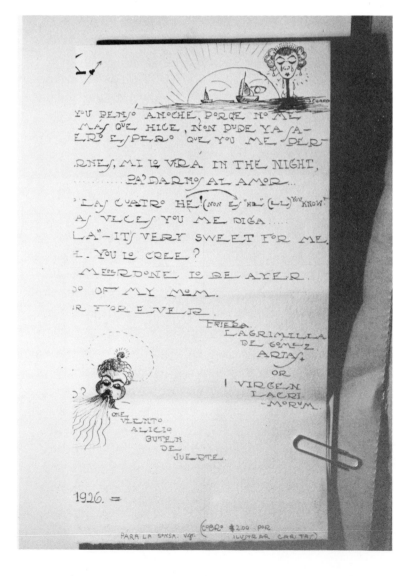

A facsimile of one of Kahlo's letters to Alejandro Gómez, written in a playful blend of Spanish and English. Though she did her best to evoke his sympathy— signing herself as "the little tear of Gómez Arias" and "the Virgin of Tears"—her former lover continued to avoid her.

1928, President Obregón was assassinated. Political power passed to a group headed by former president Plutarco Calles, and new elections were scheduled for the fall of 1929. José Vasconcelos, still the minister of education, believed that Calles was even worse than the former dictator Porfirio Díaz and decided to run for president. Vasconcelos knew he could not win against the candidate of the powerful and corrupt Calles clique—which effectively ran the country until 1934—but he hoped that a new party, dedicated to the spirit of democracy promised during the Mexican Revolution, would be born out of his campaign. Many of his supporters were students at the university.

By June 1928, Alejandro Gómez had fallen in love with another woman and made it clear that his affair with Kahlo would never be revived. For weeks Kahlo wrote pleading letters to him, but this time she apparently gave up. She had started to paint again and began to take it very seriously. She wondered whether she could earn a living from her art, whether anyone would buy her paintings. Most of her canvases during 1928 and early 1929 were portraits of family members. She attempted to paint the dreadful bus accident and managed to produce a graphic but rough depiction of the catastrophe. For the rest of her life the damage caused by the accident would dominate her haunting, strangely moving paintings.

On May 17, 1929, a nationwide student strike took place. At the University of Mexico, a large rally was broken up by police armed with firehoses and guns. But the students did not give up. After the savage attack, they opened up a campaign to make the university autonomous—separate from the government—in order to prevent future assaults. By July, with Alejandro Gómez as president of the National Student Confederation, the students won their demand. The University of Mexico became the Autonomous University of Mexico: the institution would govern itself, and the police would no longer be permitted to enter the university grounds. Kahlo was involved with many of the student activities, but she did not have the physical strength to participate fully.

During the period when Gómez was in Europe, another friend from school, Germán de Campo, had visited Kahlo frequently. Handsome and amusing, de Campo was a fervent radical, excited about developments in the Soviet Union, which had been a socialist state since the Bolshevik Revolution in 1917. He spent long hours discussing politics with Kahlo. De

Alvaro Obregón (seated at left), president of Mexico from 1920–24 and again in 1928, was a popular leader who promoted democracy and stimulated the nation's cultural life. Obregón's assassination in 1928 gave rise to a wave of student protests in which Kahlo was an eager participant.

Campo was assassinated in July 1929, as he gave a speech supporting Vasconcelos's candidacy. But during the previous year he had introduced Kahlo to a whole new world—the group that assembled weekly at the home of the Italian-born American photographer Tina Modotti.

Modotti became Kahlo's role model. She had come to Mexico a few years earlier as the protégée of the famous American photographer Edward Weston. When Weston went home, Modotti stayed, photographing the peasants of Mexico and posing for Diego Rivera. She was open and proud about her many love affairs. Her casual affair with Rivera was at least the partial cause of Rivera's breakup with Lupe Marín.

Modotti was unlike any woman Kahlo had ever met. Independent, daring, revolutionary, Modotti befriended the young painter and sponsored her membership in the Mexican Communist party. As Kahlo moved into Modotti's exciting circle of artists, writers, and intellectuals, she lost interest in student politics. She cut her hair very short and donned the red shirt of the young Communists.

At a get-together at Modotti's home, Kahlo saw Diego Rivera again. Later, he did not remember the shy young girl quietly watching the crowd of celebrities. But Kahlo was fascinated by the impetuous Rivera. In many ways they were alike. Both were outrageous pranksters and born masters of exaggeration. At one point in the festivities, for example, Rivera disliked the music. He whipped out his pistol and shot the phonograph. Kahlo was delighted. "I began to be very interested in him, in spite of the fear I had of him," she later recalled.

That interest would turn into the love of her life.

THE FROG PRINCE

When Frida Kahlo entered the Ministry of Education building clutching three of her paintings, she gazed awestruck at an amazing sight. Up to a height of three stories, the walls were covered with dozens of huge murals vividly dramatizing the history of Mexico's persecuted Indians. Diego Rivera, perched high up on the scaffolding, was putting the finishing touches on five years of labor. He did not notice the small figure on the ground floor.

Rivera had been born on December 8, 1886, in the Mexican mining city of Guanajuato. There were several striking similarities between his family background and Kahlo's. His father, also named Diego Rivera, was a schoolteacher. Like Guillermo Kahlo, he was a freethinker, of Spanish and Portuguese-Jewish descent. Diego Rivera's mother, María del Pilar Barrientos de Rivera, of Spanish and Indian ancestry like Matilde Kahlo, was also a devout Catholic.

Kahlo on the patio of the Blue House in 1930, a year after her marriage to Diego Rivera. Kahlo found little comfort in married life, but her association with Rivera was a stimulus to her art.

From the age of three, Diego longed to be an artist. He drew on the walls and furniture of his home until his father provided him with his first studio, a room with canvas-covered walls. The Rivera family moved to Mexico City when Diego was six. Four years later he convinced his parents to pay the tuition for evening classes at the San Carlos Academy, the most respected art school in Mexico City. By the time he was 13, the school awarded him a scholarship to attend days as a full-time art student. In 1903, at the age of 17, Rivera was expelled when he helped to organize a strike against the Díaz regime. He continued to paint and traveled all over Mexico.

In 1907, the same year that Frida Kahlo was born, the governor of Veracruz awarded Rivera a small grant to study art in Europe. He did not return to live in Mexico until 1921. A few years later, he became— along with José Clemente Orozco and David Alfaro Siqueiros—a leader of the internationally famous Mexican mural movement. His name was known to even the poorest and humblest people in Mexico and abroad.

Because of Rivera's international reputation, most visitors approached him with deference. Kahlo threw caution to the winds, shouting out, "Diego, come down!"

Curious to know more about the daring young girl below, the bulky Rivera made the slow descent to the ground floor. Kahlo wasted no time in preliminaries. "I have not come to flirt, and even if you are a woman chaser, I have come to show you my paintings," she told him audaciously. She told him her name, and Rivera remembered that just a few years earlier, the director of the National Preparatory had told him that the girl who had caused him so much trouble was the same Frida Kahlo. Instead of becoming angry at Kahlo's audacity, the unconventional artist was delighted to meet his former tormentor face to face.

Kahlo brusquely informed Rivera that she wanted him to tell her the unvarnished truth about her work. If she could not earn her living as an artist, she announced, she would take up some other profession to help her parents. "I want you to tell me if I am a good enough artist to make it worthwhile to go on."

Kahlo unwrapped three of her portraits and waited as Rivera studied them. In a few minutes, he informed her that she was indeed an authentic artist. Kahlo worried that Rivera was lavishing her with false praise in order to seduce her. Nevertheless, she invited him to visit her home in Coyoacán the following Sunday to see the rest of her paintings.

On his first visit to the Blue House, Rivera spotted Kahlo high up in an orange tree, dressed in overalls and whistling a revolutionary tune. The sight had a powerful effect on his emotions; he later wrote that Kahlo quickly became "the most important fact of my life."

Rivera began to make Sundays at the Kahlo home a regular event. During the week, Kahlo came often to the Ministry of Education building to watch Rivera at work and to pose for him. He painted her in the panel entitled *Distributing Arms* in his third-floor mural, *Ballad of the Proletarian Revolution*. She is shown holding a bunch of knives in one hand and a rifle in the other, her hair cropped close to her head and a red star on her work shirt. It was the first of Kahlo's many appearances in Rivera murals.

During their courtship, Kahlo painted more than ever. At first she dabbled with murals herself, but Rivera insisted that she develop her own unique style. He was willing to teach her technique, but he refused to interfere with her creative ideas. Nevertheless, his desire to immortalize the Indians of Mexico influenced Kahlo's paintings during that period. In *The Bus,* painted in 1929, the bold colors and the Indian woman with her baby were reminiscent of Rivera's style.

When Kahlo and Rivera announced that they were in love and intended to marry, Guillermo Kahlo gave his permission. His dreams of a medical career for his favorite daughter had been destroyed in seconds by the fateful trolley. His other daughters were all mar-

ried, and at 22, Frida was considered dangerously old to remain single. Furthermore, Rivera was famous, wealthy, and known for his generosity: Guillermo had found it impossible to keep up with his mortgage payments and the mountains of unpaid medical bills. He also realized that his daughter's health problems were far from over, and he did not conceal that fact from Rivera. "My daughter is a sick person and all of her life she will be sick," he bluntly told the painter. The warning had little impact. Rivera was in love with his "little girl," as he often called Frida.

Matilde Kahlo, apparently not as greedy for money as her daughter claimed, refused to approve the match. Rivera's wealth, as far as she was concerned, could not compensate for his communistic, atheistic beliefs and the fact that he was fat, homely, and too old for her daughter. Many of Kahlo's friends also tried to dissuade her from marrying the famous muralist. Some of them even asked Alejandro Gómez to attempt to stop her. No one had a chance of succeeding.

The wedding took place at the Coyoacán city hall on August 21, 1929. The town mayor performed the

The Bus, painted by Kahlo in 1929, clearly shows the influence of Rivera's murals. Although Rivera was eager to help Kahlo develop her talent, he encouraged her to create her own style as a painter.

ceremony, and three townspeople acted as witnesses. The only family member present was Guillermo Kahlo. Instead of the customary white bridal gown, Frida had borrowed a native costume from a maid and wore a special apparatus on her damaged right foot to control her limp. Disregarding the traditions of the period, she officially retained her own name.

After the ceremony, there was a lavish celebration. According to newspaper reports and Kahlo's own account, Rivera drank too much tequila and terrified the partygoers by waving his pistol around. His new bride went home and waited for him to sober up and apologize.

Shortly after the marriage, Rivera paid off the mortgage on the Blue House, and the couple moved into Rivera's impressive house on the most elegant street in Mexico City, Paseo de la Reforma. A live-in maid took care of all their daily needs, but the newlyweds had little privacy. David Siqueiros and his wife as well as two other Communist party members shared the house with them. In those first months of marriage, however, lack of privacy was the least of their problems.

For one thing, if Kahlo had thought that Rivera would spend much of his time with her, she was sadly mistaken. Before the paint was dry on his Ministry of Education murals, he launched an enormous project at the National Palace, recreating the entire history of Mexico on the building's vast interior walls. On top of this, Rivera accepted the post of director of his old art school, the San Carlos Academy. It was a prestigious position for the man who had once been expelled, and Rivera plunged into the job, making daring changes in the curriculum.

Disapproving of both of these assignments, the leaders of the Communist party denounced Rivera. Calles and his puppets ruled Mexico, and the Communists were calling for an armed uprising to restore the democratic principles of the Mexican Revolution. Rivera believed that such action would lead to defeat and bloodshed. The Communists accused him of opportunism. After all, he was receiving important commissions from the Calles regime. The fact that he painted a satirical portrait of Calles on the National Palace walls meant nothing to the Communist leaders. They wanted Rivera to boycott the Calles regime, end his friendships with government officials, and no longer sell his work to wealthy art collectors in the United States.

Pressed to resign from the party, Rivera showed up at a Communist meeting on October 3, 1929, and staged a mock expulsion, accusing himself of ridiculous crimes and waving a clay gun at the angry leaders. Kahlo sat by his side. A short while later, she joined Rivera in resigning from the party.

Kahlo and Rivera take part in a 1929 demonstration of the Syndicate of Technical Workers, Painters, and Sculptors. Though closely identified with left-wing causes, Rivera broke with the Communist party in 1929; Kahlo quickly followed suit.

Despite Rivera's bravado, the break with his old friends hurt him deeply. Most of them no longer spoke to him. The tenants at the house on La Reforma packed up and moved out. Rivera plunged back into work, not only painting at the National Palace but also at the Ministry of Health building, then rushing off in the evening to perform his duties at the art school.

Rivera had always worked from early morning until late at night, sometimes even going without sleep. When he painted, he was a man possessed. Even his many affairs had been incorporated into his painting schedule. The women who wanted him had met him where he worked, making love to him in the rooms of the buildings he was decorating. Kahlo quickly discovered that she would have no time with Rivera at all unless she stayed with him at his mural sites.

As Kahlo gradually realized that she would always be second fiddle to Rivera's art, a startling change came over her. She stopped painting and devoted all of her time to her husband. Her spirit of independence seemed to vanish. Just as she had been obsessed with Alejandro Gómez, she now focused on Diego Rivera. She took cooking lessons from his ex-wife Lupe Marín, who had remarried, and learned to prepare Rivera's favorite foods. Every day she showed up at the National Palace or wherever he was painting, carrying meals to him in baskets heaped with love notes and flowers.

Rivera seemed at first to enjoy the attention, but it quickly irritated him. He had always been a man who loved his freedom. Clinging vines were not his favorite type, and when he married the *artist* Frida Kahlo, he had not dreamed that she would play the role of devoted wife so avidly. Lupe Marín's possessiveness and jealousy had been exactly the qualities that had turned Rivera away from her. There was also the delicate question of marital fidelity. Rivera knew that he was incapable of remaining true to one woman for very long. Although he loved Kahlo, he had also loved Marín and others before and after her. He had never been able to resist temptation.

In December 1929, Dwight W. Morrow, the U.S. ambassador to Mexico, invited Rivera to paint a mural at the Hernán Cortés Palace in Cuernavaca, about 50 miles south of Mexico City. When Rivera agreed, a barrage of fresh criticism was hurled at him. Morrow had helped to negotiate agreements with the Calles government that helped the "Yanquis" steal Mexican oil, Rivera's old friends screamed. Rivera insisted that the mural would have an important political impact. He would depict the glories of the Mexican Revolution and the horrors of the Spanish Conquest.

When Ambassador Morrow and his wife went to London in late December, Rivera and Kahlo moved into the Morrows' summer home in Cuernavaca. Kahlo spent many lonely hours once again, wandering around in the gardens or watching Rivera paint at the Cortés Palace. Late at night, when she thought she would have Rivera to herself, he wanted to go out on the town with his friends and admirers. Kahlo, feeling neglected and exhausted, would often leave and go home to bed.

While she lived in Cuernavaca, Kahlo began to develop her own unique style of dress, choosing clothes that she thought would please Rivera. Since her husband was so fascinated by Mexican Indian culture, Kahlo took to wearing the costume of the Indian Tehuantepec women. Her outfits featured long skirts that hid her withered leg. She developed a fascination with jewelry, and Rivera bought her drawers full of jade, silver, and gold ornaments.

Toward the end of the year in Cuernavaca, Kahlo became pregnant. Medical opinions differed widely

Rivera's former model and ex-wife Lupe Marín, depicted in a 1930 portrait by Kahlo, taught Kahlo to cook Rivera's favorite dishes. Rivera was not entirely pleased by his new wife's attentiveness— he had expected her to pursue her career and leave him to his own devices.

on whether Kahlo should or even could bear a child. Some doctors felt that she could not go through the ordeal of labor and recommended a cesarean delivery to spare her fragile pelvis and spine. Others felt that pregnancy itself would be dangerous for her. Rivera was completely opposed to having more children; he had already sired four with three different women. He was concerned about his wife's health, of course, but he certainly did not want further responsibility. After undergoing an abortion, Kahlo wept for weeks.

Soon rumors reached Kahlo's ears that Rivera was having an affair with one of his assistants. She claimed that she did not care, that her husband expected her to have her own life and he could have his. But later she commented bitterly, "I suffered two grave accidents in my life, one in which a streetcar ran me over; the other accident is Diego."

The unhappiness that started so soon after Kahlo married Rivera would provide the subject matter for many of Kahlo's future paintings. Her canvases would not be peaceful portraits of friends or scenes of Mexico but more often nightmarish fantasies of ruined bodies and floating fetuses.

As the work on the Cuernavaca mural reached completion, Rivera and Kahlo had a decision to make. The mural renaissance was being phased out by a conservative government. Fascist bands roamed the streets defacing murals and beating up "Indian lovers." Orozco had been in exile since 1924, painting murals in the United States. Siqueiros, still an active Communist party member, had been under house arrest for three years. Rivera had no offers for new murals in Mexico and was under attack from all sides. Leftists labeled him a government spy, and rightists called him a dangerous revolutionary.

In May 1930, when he was fired by the government as director of the San Carlos Art Academy, Rivera made his decision. Tired of being hounded, he would leave his beloved Mexico and go north to the United States, where he had often been invited to paint murals.

Kahlo was overjoyed. It would be her first trip outside her native country. Her old dream of seeing San Francisco was coming true, but she would not be traveling with Alejandro Gómez, and she was not going in poverty. Her companion would be one of the world's most famous artists, and they would arrive with their pockets full of dollars.

The trip was delayed for several weeks when the U.S. Department of State refused to grant Kahlo and Rivera entry visas because of their politics. Finally, a wealthy businessman and patron of the arts pressured the State Department to permit the couple to visit.

With several assignments for Rivera already lined up, the two Mexican artists left for San Francisco, arriving in the California city on November 10, 1930. For Kahlo, reality was to be quite different from her dream.

STRANGER IN
A STRANGE LAND

Frida Kahlo's three-year nightmare in America began as an exciting adventure in San Francisco. Wealthy patrons of the arts provided the visiting Mexicans with a spacious studio, took them on whirlwind tours of the city, and wined and dined them in elegant restaurants and nightclubs.

Rivera was constantly the center of attention, and he loved every minute of it. A stranger in a strange land, Kahlo sat quietly beside her husband as he roared with laughter, told his familiar stories, drank and ate prodigiously, and flirted with every woman in sight. His audiences adored him, extolling his art and fawning over him. Reporters followed Rivera everywhere.

Kahlo received attention too, but never for her art or personality. In sophisticated San Francisco, people turned to stare admiringly at an unusual apparition on the street—23-year-old Frida Kahlo bedecked in her long skirt and petticoats, her hair piled high with ribbons and flowers, on the arm of a tall, very fat man in a cowboy hat and boots. Famous photographers invited her to their studios to sit for portraits. From the very first day, Kahlo was viewed as no more than Diego Rivera's wife, a decorative object accompany-

Kahlo and Rivera pose happily in San Francisco, where they stayed during 1930 and 1931. Visiting the City by the Bay had been a longtime dream of Kahlo's, but the reality proved disappointing: she disliked American culture and was disgusted by the extremes of wealth and poverty she saw around her.

ing the famous muralist, a delicate bird with bright
plumage next to the fat and homely man.

Not taken seriously by the art world, Kahlo had a
problem taking her own art seriously. She sketched
and painted only when there was nothing else to do.
Her dream of making her own living from her art
seemed to have evaporated.

Exploring the mansions and public buildings of
San Francisco, Rivera marveled over the sights,
sketching constantly as he extolled the virtues of
modern technology and enjoyed the company of
adoring fans. Kahlo, on the other hand, found Americans boring, hated their food and their homes, even
their faces, which she compared to "unbaked rolls,
especially the old women."

Kahlo and Rivera had arrived in the United States
in the darkest days of the Great Depression. All around
them the streets were filled with desperate unemployed men and women lining up for stale bread and
watery soup at charity kitchens, their eyes empty, their
cheeks hollow. Kahlo could not forget the dilapidated
slums as she toured the ornate homes, expensive restaurants, and elegant galleries of Rivera's money-
obsessed admirers, who continued to prosper despite
the depression.

As usual, Rivera's fascination did not end with
steel bridges and modern architecture. Charmed by
the American love of sports, he decided to make
athletics an important part of his *Allegory of California*
mural at the Pacific Stock Exchange Luncheon Club.
When he met tennis champion Helen Wills Moody,
he urged her to become his model.

Kahlo, who had tramped around with her husband to everything from theaters to football games,
was having serious problems with her right foot.
Rivera disappeared for days, and it was no secret
that he was spending his time with Moody. In mid-

January, when Rivera started around-the-clock work on his mural, Kahlo was on her own.

Knowing Rivera's preference for independent women, Kahlo did not complain. She spent time with the wives of Rivera's assistants, who had traveled north for the privilege of working for the master painter, often without pay. Kahlo toured the artsy North Beach area, sparing her foot as much as possible, and spent many hours in San Francisco's famous China-town, buying Oriental jewelry and yards of silk for her dresses.

When her foot hurt so much that she could barely walk, Kahlo checked into the San Francisco General Hospital for a brief stay. It was there that she met Dr. Leo Eloesser, a famous bone surgeon who would become her lifelong friend as well as her medical and personal adviser. A true humanitarian, Eloesser later volunteered to serve as a doctor in the Spanish Re-publican army, tending the wounded volunteers who defended the Republic against the Fascist forces dur-ing the Spanish Civil War. After the war he moved to a humble village in Michoacán, Mexico, and ran a community clinic. After he took care of Kahlo in San Francisco, she painted his portrait and presented it to him as a gift.

Rivera's mural was completed in less than a month and opened for public viewing on March 15, 1931. Invited to rest at the country home of a wealthy socialite, Rosalie Meyer Stern, Rivera and Kahlo stayed with the Sterns for six weeks. While Rivera painted a mural in the dining room as a gift for their hosts, Kahlo turned once again to her brushes and paints.

Kahlo's first fantasy painting took shape—a mini-ature portrait of the famous plant geneticist Luther Burbank. Burbank emerged on the canvas as half-tree, half-man. This startling concept may have been in-

One of the few benefits of Kahlo's stay in the United States was her friendship with Dr. Leo Eloesser, whose portrait she painted in 1931. A political idealist and a brilliant bone surgeon, Eloesser became Kahlo's lifelong friend and medical adviser.

spired by Kahlo's interest in surrealism, a style of painting that abandoned ordinary logic for dream images. On the other hand, she might have taken her cue from Rivera: he had included Burbank in the Stock Exchange mural and at the Agricultural School mural in Chapingo, Mexico, where he had drawn Tina Modotti's nude body fading into the trunk of a tree.

At the end of April 1931, Kahlo and Rivera returned to San Francisco, where Rivera started his work at the California School of Fine Arts. Once again, Kahlo was alone much of the time. Sick of touring the city, she continued to paint. Out of her loneliness, she worked on a wedding portrait, *Frida and Diego Rivera,* using Rivera's name on a canvas for the first time.

When Kahlo accompanied Rivera on his many nights out, she saw that he was always drawn to women who were outgoing, active, and talkative. Since Rivera did not seem to notice her when she was ill or depressed and withdrawn, Kahlo forced herself to move into the limelight. After all, she had been a mischievous and outrageous Cachucha when he fell in love with her. She became a crowd pleaser, singing bawdy Mexican songs, flirting with the men, and engaging in sparkling conversation. Rivera immediately refocused his attention on her, and she was briefly happier.

Most of all, though, Kahlo longed for home. Her husband did not seem to care if he never saw Mexico again. But by June 1931, when his second mural was completed, Rivera finally agreed to leave the United States. The Mexican government had been urging him to return to finish the National Palace stairway murals, and a happy Kahlo flew home with him to Mexico City.

It seemed that now they would stay put. They moved in with Kahlo's parents at the Blue House in Coyoacán, and with the money from the San Francisco projects, they began construction on a new home in Mexico City's fashionable San Angel neighborhood.

Kahlo's happiness lasted less than six months. An emissary from the Museum of Modern Art in New York City arrived to invite Rivera to exhibit his work in a one-person show, only the second ever held in the prestigious museum. The idea had been born in the living room of the wealthy Rockefeller family, participants in the U.S.-Mexican Arts Association, an organization attempting to encourage friendship and cultural exchanges between the two countries. It did not seem to bother the Rockefellers that Rivera was an outspoken opponent of capitalism. After all, if the Calles government could sponsor his art, why not the Museum of Modern Art? The catalog for the exhibit assured the public that "Diego's very spinal column is painting, not politics."

With the National Palace mural still incomplete, Rivera and Kahlo sailed for New York in mid-November. For Rivera, New York City outdid even San Francisco. He bellowed with joy when he saw the famous New York skyline from the ship's deck. The crowds were even more adoring; the technology even more impressive. But Kahlo could not help but notice that there were also more poor people on the city's crowded streets.

Kahlo and Rivera were installed in plush quarters at the Hotel Barbizon Plaza, with windows looking down on Central Park. There was an endless chain of parties and receptions, with wealthy high society patrons on hand to greet them. Once again Rivera was in his element. Kahlo wrote to Leo Eloesser: "I feel a bit of rage against all these rich guys here, since I have seen thousands of people in the most terrible misery without anything to eat and with no place to sleep. ...It is terrifying to see the rich having parties day and night while thousands of people are dying of hunger. . . . I find that Americans completely lack sensibility and good taste."

Rivera had less than a month to prepare his show, and Kahlo complained to Eloesser, "I, as always, never do anything except look and get bored." Rivera was constantly surrounded by women, and Kahlo could not easily conceal her jealousy. At one dinner party, Rivera spent the evening in earnest conversation with Lucienne Bloch, an artist of Swiss ancestry. Kahlo was seated too far away to hear their words, but she

Kahlo and Rivera embrace in the Garden Court of the Detroit Institute of Arts, where Rivera undertook a mural project in 1932. Despite the peaceful and romantic atmosphere of this scene, the couple's stay in the Motor City was a torment for Kahlo.

became convinced that Bloch would be Rivera's next amorous adventure. When the two women were introduced after dinner, Kahlo startled Bloch by blurting out, "I hate you!" Bloch went out of her way to assure Kahlo that she had no romantic interest in Rivera, and the two women soon became fast friends.

Rivera's opening on December 22, 1931, was one of the most publicized events of the year. Kahlo delighted the elite crowd of invitees with her Tehuana costume, and the critics raved over Rivera's work. In the following weeks, Kahlo attended dozens of concerts and plays, enjoying few of them. She never developed a taste for classical music. While Rivera held forth at the Museum of Modern Art, she enjoyed entertainment more to her liking, horror movies like *Frankenstein* and slapstick films featuring Laurel and Hardy and the Marx Brothers. By the time Rivera's show closed on January 27, 1932, Kahlo had had enough of New York.

This time, she was not displeased that Rivera was on the move again: the Institute of Arts in Detroit, Michigan, invited him to paint a mural. By the end of April the couple was in Detroit, ensconced in an old hotel opposite the institute. By that time, news of Adolf Hitler's campaign against the Jews in Nazi Germany was common knowledge. Kahlo expressed her disgust with the German anti-Semitism by introducing herself as Carmen Kahlo, using her middle name instead of her Germanic first name. When she and Rivera discovered that the hotel did not accept Jewish guests, they told the manager that they were Jewish and threatened to leave if the ban was not lifted. Business was bad in depression-ravaged Detroit, and the manager immediately granted their demand.

Despite the conservative climate in Detroit, Rivera was delighted by the auto-making city. With a reluctant Kahlo by his side, he toured the Ford Motor Company's River Rouge plant in nearby Dearborn, sketching happily. The sight of the production lines delighted him. His fascination with technology increased. The 27 fresco panels for the Art Institute's Garden Court were planned as a celebration of the Motor City's industry. Kahlo found Detroit gloomy, the plants noisy and unpleasant.

Kahlo was even more miserable than she had been in New York or San Francisco. People again stared at her on the street, but now in shock rather than admiration. The elite of Detroit had none of the sophistication of the wealthy San Franciscans and New Yorkers. They flattered Rivera but ignored Kahlo completely, making no secret of the fact that they thought her outfits idiotic. In the spirit of revenge,

Kahlo used four-letter words liberally and spoke loudly against capitalism and for socialism. Around religious people, she criticized the church. When she accompanied Rivera to the elegant mansion of Henry Ford, the owner of the Ford Motor Company and the author of a notorious anti-Semitic tract, *International Jew,* she loudly asked him if he was Jewish.

A few weeks after arriving in Detroit, Kahlo discovered that she was pregnant again. With Rivera still adamantly opposed to having more children and with her own health always precarious, Kahlo attempted to obtain an abortion, then illegal in the United States. On May 26, she asked Dr. Eloesser to contact the physician she was seeing in Detroit. If Eloesser could convince the authorities that Kahlo's life would be endangered by pregnancy, she would be able to have a safe hospital abortion.

Eloesser complied, but during the intervening weeks, Kahlo decided to try to have the child despite

Kahlo at work in Detroit in 1932. Her three-year visit to the United States with Rivera was an ordeal for Kahlo: while he was wined and dined, she was expected to play the role of the great man's adoring wife, and few Americans took her seriously as an artist.

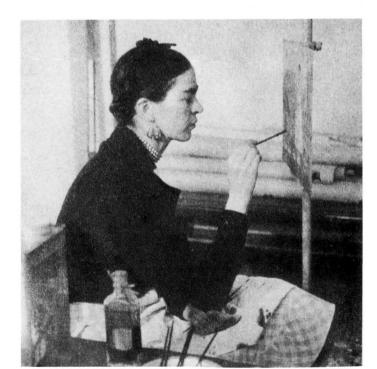

the obstacles. Unable to dissuade her, Rivera convinced Lucienne Bloch to come and stay with Kahlo: he himself would be too busy with his new mural to spend the necessary time with her. Bloch loyally agreed; she slept in the living room and spent her days encouraging Kahlo to paint.

Detroit was extremely hot during the summer of 1932, and Kahlo consistently disobeyed her doctor's orders to rest. On July 4, she woke up at dawn, hemorrhaging severely. A terrified Rivera comforted her while Bloch called an ambulance that rushed Kahlo to Henry Ford Hospital. After a painful miscarriage and almost two weeks of hemorrhaging and depression, a thin and exhausted Kahlo returned to the hotel apartment. Six days later Rivera started his mural at the Art Institute.

Her sufferings inspired Kahlo to paint in earnest. *Henry Ford Hospital,* dated July 1932, marked the emergence of the distinctive style that would eventually bring her fame. Rembembering that Mexican church walls were often decorated with stories painted on tin, called ex-votos or *retablos,* Kahlo decided to let her tiny paintings tell stories too. And what stories! *Henry Ford Hospital* was the first of Kahlo's many bloody and horrific self-portraits, depicting scenes never before publicly shown in a still-puritanical United States, where even in the movies, married couples were not permitted to be shown asleep in the same bed. *Henry Ford Hospital* depicts Kahlo lying nude in a pool of blood on a hospital bed. A large tear rolls down one side of her expressionless face. She is surrounded by a strange collection of objects: a baby boy, a pregnant woman, a drawing of a pelvis from a medical textbook, a machine, and a purple orchid. Rivera called the painting "agonized poetry."

(Continued on page 73)

The Paintings of
Frida Kahlo

Self-Portrait (1930)

66

Fruits of the Earth (1938)

Luther Burbank (1931)

Self-Portrait with Small Monkey (1945)

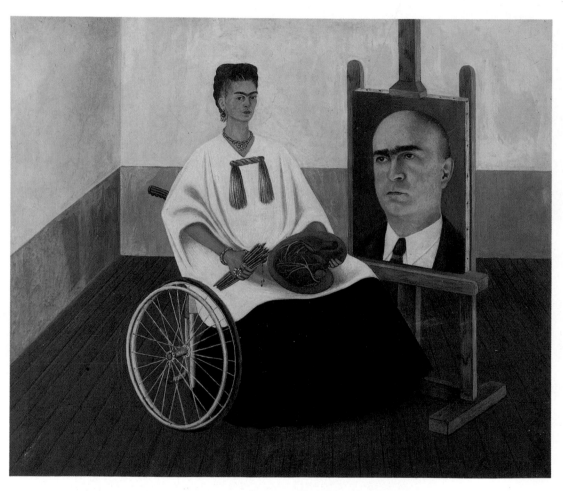

Self-Portrait with the Portrait of Dr. Farill (1951)

The Two Fridas (1939)

Tree of Hope (1946)

(Continued from page 64)

When Kahlo recovered her strength, she tried other media for her work, including lithography. Her strikingly original style continued to emerge. Several paintings, such as *Self-Portrait on the Border Line Between Mexico and the United States,* expressed her longing for home and her dislike of American culture: Aztec pyramids contrasted with Detroit smokestacks; machines and plants battled for supremacy.

As soon as she was able to, Kahlo once again brought Rivera his lunch at the Art Institute every day. He was on a vegetarian diet, trying hard to lose weight, and she monitored his progress carefully. Her yearning for Mexico increased with each passing day. "I am not happy here, but I have to pluck up my courage and stay because I cannot leave Diego," she confided to Eloesser.

On September 3, 1932, however, a telegram from her sisters informed Kahlo that her mother was dying. With Bloch for company, Kahlo boarded a train and arrived in Mexico City after an arduous five-day journey.

On September 15, Matilde Kahlo died, surrounded by her grieving daughters. Kahlo stayed in Coyoacán five more weeks, attempting to comfort her ailing 60-year-old father, but she worried about Rivera, on the loose in Detroit. She returned on October 21. Rivera was at the station waiting for her. He had lost almost 100 pounds, and Kahlo barely recognized him.

De-energized and ill, Rivera became even more difficult to live with. For one thing, he let Kahlo know immediately that he had no intention of returning to Mexico when his work in Detroit was completed. Other invitations had poured in. He had been chosen to paint a mural in the main lobby of the RCA Building, in Rockefeller Center in New York City, as well as another for the upcoming 1933 World's Fair in Chicago. It seemed that Rivera had every intention of living in the United States forever.

Kahlo spent five more miserable months in Detroit. During this period, with little else to distract her, she worked hard on her painting. Continuing in the same vein as *Henry Ford Hospital,* she created another terrifying portrait entitled *My Birth.* Still, she did not consider herself a genuine painter and never imagined that anyone would be interested in buying her work. She felt that she painted purely for personal satisfaction. Her self-confidence was not increased when the *Detroit News* printed an interview she had granted them under the insulting headline WIFE OF THE MASTER MURAL PAINTER GLEEFULLY DABBLES IN WORKS OF ART.

In late March 1933, Rivera completed the Art Institute mural, and he and Kahlo returned to New York and the plush Barbizon Plaza. Kahlo seemed resigned to the situation. New York, after all, was more interesting than Detroit. At Rockefeller Center, hundreds of people bought tickets to watch Rivera work. Kahlo began to visit the work site several times a week, usually in the evening when the crowds were gone. During the day, she went on long shopping expeditions to the best stores and began to wear high fashion outfits instead of her native costume. Lucienne Bloch—who was now married to one of Rivera's assistants, Stephen Dimitroff—tried to persuade Kahlo to paint, but she could not seem to concentrate: for nine months, she did not complete a single work.

On April 24, when Rivera's vast mural, *Man at the Crossroads,* was two-thirds complete, a scandal broke out. The conservative press started the fracas, complaining about the inclusion of "Communist" themes in the work. Rivera's mural did indeed include Socialist themes, because he considered socialism one of the

Kahlo painted Self-Portrait on the Border Line Between Mexico and the United States *in 1932, during her stay in Detroit. The painting vividly contrasts the mechanized culture of the United States with the fertile, mythic allure of Mexico; the Mexican flag in Kahlo's hand clearly indicates her preference.*

legitimate options for the world's peoples. Capitalism in the West and socialism in the East were world realities. Abby Rockefeller, then married to John D. Rockefeller, Jr., the billionaire who was paying the bills, came often to see Rivera's work and had nothing but praise for it.

The tempest escalated when Rivera painted the face of Vladimir Lenin, one of the leaders of the Russian Revolution, into his mural. This was too much for the Rockefellers. Rivera offered to put Abraham Lincoln into the mural, but there was no compromise possible—Lenin had to go. Rivera refused to submit to censorship; on May 9, the Rockefellers fired him and had the mural covered up. This action evoked a storm of protest from artists and all those favoring free expression. Pickets marched in front of Rockefeller Center and the Rockefeller mansion. Kahlo, deeply indignant, typed dozens of letters to potential supporters and attended all the protest meetings and rallies. In a symbolic gesture, she tossed aside her elegant wardrobe and donned her Tehuana dresses again.

As a result of the controversy, Rivera's other promised mural contracts were canceled. Kahlo hoped that now there would be no reason to stay in the United States, but again she was disappointed. Rivera, in a foul mood, said that Mexico was even worse. He decided to use his severance pay from the Rockefellers to finance a mural at the New Workers School in New York, depicting the history of the United States. The New Workers School was run by a group of Trotskyites. The Trotskyites believed that the current leader of the Soviet Union, Joseph Stalin, had betrayed the Russian Revolution; they supported Leon Trotsky, the former leader of the Red Army, who had been expelled from the Soviet Union by Stalin. Rivera knew that his association with the Trotskyites would infuriate his Communist party friends, but he seemed to enjoy that idea.

The New Workers School was about to be torn down, so Rivera painted on movable panels, portraying champions of the oppressed, such as Lincoln and the antislavery crusader John Brown. One panel that would later prove explosive depicted "Stalin the Executioner" standing behind the figures of Lenin and Trotsky.

No longer able to afford their luxury hotel, Rivera and Kahlo moved into a Greenwich Village apartment. Before long, Rivera became romantically involved with a neighbor, the well-known sculptor Louise

Nevelson. The old pattern continued. Whenever Rivera was depressed, he looked to other women for solace, and Kahlo responded by falling ill. This time, her right foot appeared to be paralyzed, and she was unable to walk. The apartment was terribly hot in the summer, and Kahlo convinced Rivera to move into the Brevoort Hotel on lower Fifth Avenue, perhaps hoping to get him away from Nevelson. With Kahlo openly in misery, Rivera asked friends to convince her to paint again.

Kahlo wanted only to go home. The couple argued bitterly. Rivera claimed he wanted to stay in the United States, despite the censorship, because the Socialist revolution was bound to start there. He was deeply impressed that workers had demonstrated on his behalf when his mural was canceled. Kahlo disagreed. Only a comparatively small number of workers had even cared about Rivera's mural, she argued. Capitalism would find a way to bail itself out.

When Kahlo finally took up her brush, it was to create a parable about her homesickness and her loathing of the United States. In the painting entitled *My Dress Hangs There,* one of her Tehuana dresses hangs on a clothesline suspended between an athletic trophy and a toilet bowl. The composition includes boxlike apartment houses, industrial smokestacks, a church with a dollar sign on its stained-glass window, masses of unemployed men, and an overflowing garbage pail. Kahlo herself is absent.

In December 1933, Rivera's New Workers School panels were finished, and the Rockefeller money was gone. For three days in a row, Rivera presided at public showings of the mural and lectured on the subject of revolution. Meanwhile, friends took up a collection and bought the couple two boat tickets to Mexico. Raging and fuming, a reluctant Rivera boarded the steamship with Kahlo by his side.

"A Few
Small Nips"

Cristina Kahlo, in a 1928 portrait by her sister Frida. Rivera's affair with Cristina may have been the cruelest of the many wounds he inflicted upon his wife. "The more I loved [Frida], the more I wanted to hurt her," he later confessed.

Early in 1934, Kahlo and Rivera moved into their new home in San Angel. There were actually two buildings, a spacious orange-pink one for Rivera and a smaller blue one for Kahlo. A walkway connecting the upper floors was the only link between the artists' separate residences.

Like the design of their home, the couple's life together rapidly became divided. Rivera missed the United States, where in spite of his difficulties he had been surrounded by friends and admirers. In Mexico, his former friends stepped up their attacks on him, calling him a Trotskyite, a betrayer of the revolution, a painter for the rich. Moreover, Mexico's mural renaissance was over. American collectors were willing to pay outrageous prices for anything bearing Rivera's signature, but creating wondrous public walls was the work that made him happiest.

In February, word came that the unthinkable had happened. With Rivera thousands of miles away, the Rockefellers ordered workmen to smash his controversial mural into a thousand pieces. Rivera was understandably furious, and Kahlo became the focus of his anger. Blaming her for his unhappy situation,

79

Rivera declared that he hated all of his work. As his spirits sagged, his body broke down too. He suffered from eye infections and kidney ailments.

In a state of abysmal loneliness, Kahlo turned to her sister Cristina for comfort. Cristina's husband had left her in 1930, and she had moved back to the family home in Coyoacán, where she cared for her two children and her father. As always, Kahlo confided in her sister, telling her of the effect Rivera's misery had on her.

When Rivera took the advice of a doctor and gained back some of the weight he had lost, he began to feel better. A little work also trickled in, but his behavior toward Kahlo did not improve. As usual, Rivera sought to solve his problems by turning to another woman. His sister-in-law, Cristina Kahlo, was close at hand, warm and comforting. It is not certain exactly when Kahlo discovered that her husband and favorite sister were romantically involved, but Rivera made no real effort to hide the affair. Years later he told his biographer, "The more I loved [Frida], the more I wanted to hurt her."

In June 1934, Rivera was given permission to repaint a smaller version of his destroyed mural at the Palace of Fine Arts in Mexico City. Cristina Kahlo was seen often at the mural site, posing and chatting with Rivera. Frida reacted as she always had, falling prey to physical problems and not painting at all. She spent many weeks in the hospital, first with surgery to remove her appendix, then undergoing the first of many operations to relieve the pain in her right foot. She also suffered a miscarriage, her third.

When Rivera rented a luxury apartment for Cristina and furnished it in the latest mode, Kahlo knew that things would never be the same. Some of her married woman friends had taken separate living quarters and were struggling to earn independent livings. She decided to make a similar effort. With money from Rivera, she set up a small apartment in downtown Mexico City and even consulted a lawyer about a divorce. But because she continued to hope that Rivera would weary of his romance with her sister, she took no further action.

Despite her move toward independence, Kahlo's confidence was shaken. In letters to close friends, she confessed to feeling that she was "not worth two cents" without Rivera. Her paints and brushes were on hand, but work did not come easily. During all of 1935, she produced only two paintings, *Self-Portrait with Curly Hair,* showing a sorrowful Kahlo with a new haircut, and *A Few Small Nips,* an obvious message to her husband and sister. The canvas depicts a brutal man with a knife standing over a nude dead woman, her flesh riddled with bloody gashes. Above them, two birds carry a banner with the words "A few small nips!" Kahlo said the painting had been inspired by a newspaper story about a man who had murdered his sweetheart and then told the judge, "But I only gave her a few small nips!" Despite this disclaimer, the reference to Kahlo's own situation could not have been clearer. Later, she added splotches of red paint to the wooden frame of the painting.

In public, Kahlo put on a happy face. She went out frequently, laughing loudly and telling stories with her openly sexual black humor, charming everyone around her. Only a few close friends knew the depth of her unhappiness.

In July, on a sudden impulse, Kahlo jumped into a small private airplane with two women she had met the night before and headed for New York. After six days of forced landings and terrifying hours in the air, they took a train for the rest of the journey. When she reached New York, Kahlo spent hours talking to Lucienne Bloch and wrote a long letter to Rivera. She agreed to accept his infidelities, declaring that "I love you more than my own skin, and . . . though you may not love me in the same way, you still love me somewhat, isn't that so? . . . I shall always hope that that continues, and with that I am content."

Rivera agreed to a reconciliation, and Kahlo rushed back to San Angel. The couple then agreed to have an "open" marriage, which after all was already a fact. Each of them could have outside affairs, but these liaisons were, supposedly, not to interfere with their love for one another.

On the surface, Kahlo appeared to accept the new situation. She even forgave her sister and made Cristina and her children an important part of her life again. She was seen around town several times a week, at the circus, movies, boxing matches, and a small working-class bar with a dance band. She was almost always the center of attention. Her San Angel home became a gathering place for prominent artists and

Kahlo and Rivera built these twin houses in Mexico City's San Angel quarter shortly after their marriage. The arrangement was intended to provide creative privacy for the two painters—before long, the divided structures came to symbolize the couple's emotional separation.

writers from all over the globe. Kahlo held court in her beautiful native costumes and pounds of jewelry, behaving much as she had in her Cachucha days—flirting and having affairs with both men and women. But it was obvious that she was drinking heavily, even carrying a personal flask of brandy around with her.

Although Rivera spent days traveling about with visiting tourists, he watched Kahlo closely. His political enemies mocked him because of his wife's infidelities. In Mexico, as in most of the world, it was considered a feather in a man's cap to collect lovers but a disgrace if his wife did the same. Rivera's jealousy sometimes led to embarrassing scenes. On one occasion, he burst into the Blue House while Kahlo was entertaining one of her lovers, the sculptor Isamu Noguchi. While Rivera blustered and waved his pistol about, Noguchi managed to climb onto an orange tree and make his escape over the roof.

Whatever their personal conflicts, Rivera genuincly believed that Kahlo was a wonderful artist, and he encouraged her to paint and to show her work to the art world. Although she was reluctant to allow others to see her very personal canvases, she did begin to spend more time painting. Between 1937 and 1939, Kahlo produced about 20 new works. Her emotional and physical pain were still the main subjects. Privately, she told friends that she was lazy and only used her physical limitations as an excuse to loaf.

Despite their various affairs, Rivera and Kahlo stuck to their agreement to remain close friends. Since Kahlo's painting earned no income, Rivera was the sole provider. Kahlo skillfully handled the muralist's complicated finances and managed the household.

Shared reactions to world events also helped to keep the couple together. The political situation in Mexico had changed with the election of President Lázaro Cárdenas in 1934. Cárdenas surprised everyone by refusing to be simply another puppet of the

What the Water Gave Me, *painted in 1938, is a dazzling summary of the themes that domi-nate Kahlo's work. Although she was still reluctant to exhibit her paintings, Kahlo was gaining confidence as an artist and produced 20 canvases between 1937 and 1939.*

Calles political machine. In 1936, he expelled Calles from the country and launched a series of economic and political reforms, culminating in the nationalization of Mexico's oil resources in 1938. The Communist party became one of Cárdenas's most ardent supporters. Because Cárdenas sought good relations with all of the warring factions on the left, he maintained his contacts with Rivera and Kahlo, even visiting their San Angel home; at the same time, he kept the peace with Communist leaders by offering very few commissions to Rivera, the avowed Trotskyite.

On July 18, 1936, a more urgent event than the squabbling of left-wing groups shook the world: the democratic Republic of Spain was invaded by Fascist forces under the command of General Francisco Franco. Adolf Hitler's Nazi Germany and Benito Mussolini's Fascist Italy decided to test their troops and weapons by helping Franco to win power in Spain. Just as they had ignored the rise of fascism in Italy and Germany, the United States and other Western governments signed a neutrality agreement and refused aid to the beleaguered Spanish democracy. In response, volunteers from all over the world went to fight in defense of the Spanish Republic. Kahlo herself told friends that she longed to go. Instead, she and Rivera helped organize a committee to raise funds to aid the Loyalists, the anti-Fascist fighters of Spain. The two artists made speeches, organized fundraisers, and contacted influential friends.

The struggle in Spain brought Kahlo and Rivera closer than they had been since their long sojourn in the United States. But another political drama was about to unfold, and this one would drive a permanent wedge between them.

"A RIBBON
AROUND A BOMB"

I n February 1938, when Frida Kahlo was beginning to achieve recognition as an artist in her own right, she linked her success with Leon Trotsky's arrival in Mexico, calling this event "the best thing that ever happened to me in my life."

Leon Trotsky, exiled from the Soviet Union in 1928 by the brutal regime of Joseph Stalin, had spent nine years wandering the globe with his wife, Natalia Sedova Trotsky. Never abandoning his dream of socialism, Trotsky fueled the flames of Stalin's wrath by exposing Stalin's "betrayal" of the ideals of the Russian Revolution. Because his life was threatened by Stalin's agents, Trotsky and his wife were often forced to flee from one country to another.

Approached by Trotsky's desperate supporters toward the end of 1936, Diego Rivera pleaded with President Cárdenas to offer political asylum to the famous Russian revolutionary and his entourage. Rivera assured Cárdenas that he and Kahlo would house the refugees. Cárdenas consented on condition that Trotsky stay out of Mexican politics.

On January 9, 1937, a Norwegian steamship with Leon and Natalia Trotsky aboard arrived in Tampico,

Remembrance of an Open Wound, painted in 1938, reflects the physical and emotional suffering Kahlo experienced at the time. Despite her unhappiness and her continued insecurity as an artist, growing recognition of her work inspired her to paint with new energy.

87

Mexico. Rivera was hospitalized with a kidney infection, but Kahlo was part of the welcoming committee. The Trotskys were quickly whisked away on a secret train and taken to a welcoming party at the Blue House in Coyoacán.

The Blue House soon resembled a fortress, with loyal Trotskyites and Mexican police standing guard around the clock against Stalinist assassins. The windows were bricked over. Rivera even went so far as to purchase the house next door, evicting the tenants, to make sure that there was no threat from neighbors. Kahlo sent one of her own trusted servants to take care of the Trotskys.

Soon Natalia Trotsky succumbed to an attack of malaria, and Rivera returned to the hospital with recurrent kidney problems. Kahlo, feeling physically well during this period except for her always troublesome foot, kept Trotsky company much of the time. She showed him her paintings, something she rarely did with anyone, and he expressed tremendous admiration for her work. Kahlo was no doubt delighted to be in the company of so famous a man—the former head of the Red Army and, along with Lenin, the leader of the 1917 revolution that had ended the rule of the tsars in Russia and transformed the nation into the Soviet Union. Unlike the noisy, bohemian men Kahlo usually flirted with, Trotsky was reserved, courtly, and gallant—a European gentleman. Trotsky was called the Old Man by his comrades, not a comment on his age but on his vast store of knowledge. Kahlo translated the nickname into Spanish, fondly labeling him El Viejo. In fact, the 57-year-old revolutionary walked with a confident military stride that belied his years. Endowed with a powerful intellect, he loved to discuss world events and many other subjects, his voice resonant and his eyes sparkling with passion.

The Trotskys had two sons. One of them, Sergei, had remained in the Soviet Union and had been sent to a labor camp in the frigid wastes of Siberia. It was later revealed that during Trotsky's sham trial, Sergei had been brought to Moscow and charged with following his father's orders to murder several workers in the plant where he worked. Sergei refused to confess to such preposterous charges. News arrived in Mexico that Sergei Trotsky was dead, most probably executed after the trumped-up trials. Sergei's brother, Lyova, was in Paris, attempting to organize the official Socialist opposition to Stalin's regime. He lived under the constant danger of assassination.

After 35 years as a revolutionary's wife, Natalia Trotsky, at 55, was breaking down under the strain. The terrible ordeals she had shared with her husband had aged her prematurely. Trotsky himself described their emotional state at the time: "We wandered about in our little tropical gardens . . . each with a hole in his forehead."

As the flirtation between Trotsky and Kahlo escalated, Natalia Trotsky was at a distinct disadvantage. How could she compete with the exotic and talented 29-year-old artist, babbling in English with Trotsky, flirting and cavorting outrageously. "All my love," Kahlo would sing out to Trotsky when they parted, blowing him a teasing kiss. Though Kahlo's later admirers labeled her a feminist, nowhere in her many letters to friends or in her diaries did she express any awareness of the pain she was causing another woman.

Before long, the coy antics of Trotsky and Kahlo blossomed into a full-fledged affair. In front of Rivera and his own wife, Trotsky passed political books to Kahlo with love notes inside. Kahlo's battered and insatiable ego was deeply gratified. The man whom Rivera admired more than any other in the world was in love with her.

Trotsky and Kahlo met secretly at Cristina Kahlo's new house, but it was impossible to conceal their activities. After all, Trotsky was always closely guarded.

His supporters worried about the political conse-
quences of his involvement with Kahlo. The Stalinists
would love a juicy scandal about their archenemy.
Nothing would give them more pleasure than an
opportunity to smear his name. By the end of June,
Natalia Trotsky wrote cautious notes to her husband
indicating that she knew what was happening, while
Rivera either pretended ignorance or genuinely was
unaware of his wife's improbable choice of a new
lover.

In early July, Trotsky's guards whisked him into the
countryside, 80 miles away from Mexico City. Kahlo
went to visit him a few days later. Apparently, she
announced that she wanted to end the affair. Not too
long after that, Trotsky wrote a nine-page letter to
Kahlo, begging her not to break with him. He also
wrote a note to his wife, telling her that Kahlo meant
nothing to him.

Kahlo sent Trotsky's letter to Ella Wolfe, the wife of
Rivera's eventual biographer Bertram Wolfe, telling
her to destroy it. "I am very tired of the Old Man," she
commented. Trotsky, after making peace with his wife
through a series of long and humble love letters,
returned to Coyoacán on July 26.

To all appearances, the two couples remained
friends, but Kahlo could not resist reminding Trotsky
of their liaison. On November 7, 1937, Trotsky's birthday, Kahlo presented him with a painting she titled
Self-Portrait (Dedicated to Leon Trotsky). Different from
her usually bloody self-portraits, the painting showed
Kahlo in an elegant gown and shawl, framed by luxurious white curtains. With a dignified and aristocratic
air, she holds a bouquet of flowers in one hand; in her
other hand is a sheet of paper bearing the inscription
"Para Leon Trotsky con todo cariño" (For Leon Trotsky with all my love). Later, an art critic called Kahlo's
gift "a ribbon around a bomb."

Exiled by the Soviet state he had done so much to create, Leon Trotsky, shown here at left giving a speech in Denmark, was granted political asylum in Mexico in 1937. Living in the Blue House as guests of the Riveras, Trotsky soon found himself romantically involved with Kahlo.

Three months later, the Trotskys learned that their surviving son, Lyova, had died under suspicious circumstances in Paris, betrayed by his only friend. Her children dead, her wound still fresh from her husband's philandering, Natalia Trotsky wandered the Blue House like a ghost.

One beneficial effect of the Trotsky-Kahlo affair was quickly apparent. Trotsky's high opinion of Kahlo's art seemed to inspire her to return to painting in a serious fashion. "I have spent my life up until now loving Diego and being a good for nothing in respect to work, but I am now painting seriously," she wrote to Lucienne Bloch. However, Kahlo's work during this period suggests that the earlier romance between Rivera and her sister continued to hurt her deeply. In

Remembrance of an Open Wound, dated 1938, Kahlo sits in a chair with her bandaged foot on a pillow and her skirt pulled up to reveal a bloody gash in her left thigh.

Rivera, who told people that his wife was an artistic genius, encouraged Kahlo to accept an invitation to show some of her paintings at the University of Mexico's art gallery. She finally agreed, but wrote to Bloch that the gallery was a "small and rotten place" that would take "any kind of stuff."

Although she made very little effort to advance her own career, word of Kahlo's talent was slowly spreading. About a dozen of her paintings were displayed at the university gallery in November 1938. Just before the show, Edward G. Robinson, Hollywood's celebrated star of gangster movies and a devoted art collector, came to Mexico to see Rivera's murals. On the sly, Rivera showed Robinson some of Kahlo's paintings, and Robinson bought four of them, paying $200 each.

Kahlo was elated. At the age of 31 she felt financially liberated for the first time. Now she could be free, she told friends, she could go places "without asking Diego for money." She still wore her insecurities on her sleeve, frequently telling friends that she "felt sorry for purchasers" of her paintings because they could get something better for their money. Some of the buyers, she often added, only bought her works because they were in love with her.

Despite her lingering doubts, Kahlo's exhibit changed her artistic future. Julien Levy, an American art dealer with a prestigious gallery on New York City's fashionable East 57th Street, was told about Kahlo's astonishing paintings and asked for photographs. A handsome Hungarian-born photographer, Nickolas Muray, who later became Kahlo's lover, took pictures of Kahlo's work and sent them to Levy. The gallery owner was deeply impressed and asked Kahlo to submit 30 of her paintings for a show at his gallery.

Muray helped her pack and ship her paintings to New York.

Rivera was delighted at Kahlo's success, writing dozens of letters of introduction for her trip to New York and drawing up a guest list of prominent people for the opening. The French poet André Breton, a leader of the surrealist movement, heard about the upcoming New York show and invited Kahlo to exhibit her paintings in Paris. He also added considerable prestige to the New York show by writing an extremely flattering brochure about Kahlo.

In early October 1938, Kahlo arrived in New York. She seemed bright-eyed and high-spirited as she told Levy that she was permanently separated from Rivera. But no two people heard the same story. Kahlo would tell one friend that she adored Rivera. An hour or two later, she would tell someone else that he was an "old, fat pig." She would tell yet another person that she no longer loved Rivera but still cared about him. No one had any idea of what her true feelings were.

Kahlo's exhibit was well attended. Although many came to the gallery to see the wife of the infamous Diego Rivera, critics proclaimed her a significant painter in her own right. Twenty-five of her paintings were on display, from her old portrait of Luther Burbank to her gruesome *Henry Ford Hospital* and more recent terrifying self-portraits. Some of the reviewers patronized her, calling her "little Frida Kahlo" and saying that she had been too shy to show her work before. Some mocked her for insisting on using her maiden name, but they went on to rave about her talent. Only a few reviews were truly unfavorable. The critic from the staid *New York Times,* for example, jibed that Kahlo's paintings were "more obstetrical than aesthetic."

In letters to friends, Kahlo claimed that all of her paintings had been bought. Actually, an impressive number were sold, but far from all. Staying again at the elegant Barbizon Plaza, Kahlo went out frequently, charming everyone she met. Her aching right foot prevented her from walking too far, but she did tour Harlem and Little Italy. She delighted in the fact that she was frequently followed on the street because of her unusual getup. Now she wore only long skirts because, as she told one friend, "my sick leg is so ugly." Most often, she sat at a café near Central Park, watching passersby watch her. As usual, she was not starved for male companionship, enjoying flings with both Julien Levy and Nickolas Muray.

Kahlo sailed for a troubled Europe in January 1939, and stayed with the Bretons in Paris, where she was due to have an exhibition. Every politically astute person expected war. In Spain, the hated Franco in–

The Wounded Table, *painted after Kahlo's 1939 divorce from Rivera, was one of her most original works. The painting adds credence to Rivera's claim that Kahlo did her best work during the couple's two-year separation; Kahlo, on the other hand, called the period "the worst in my whole life."*

surgents were on the verge of victory. Kahlo and her friends dreaded the bloodbath that they knew Franco would initiate against those who had defended the democratic Republic. In the same way that they had abandoned Spain to the Fascists, the French and British governments had refused to defend Czechoslovakia against Nazi Germany's invasion, handing that tiny country over to Hitler in the vain hope of achieving peace. Paris trembled at the thought of a German onslaught. No one was terribly interested in art exhibits or other forms of diversion.

Thousands of refugees from Spain had flooded across the Pyrenees into France. They were penned up in huge concentration camps, living under intolerable conditions while the French government tried to decide what to do with them. Kahlo visited the camps and was horrified by the plight of the refugees. She immediately contacted Rivera, and with his help, she managed to get 400 Spanish refugees to Mexico. When her exhibit was delayed, Kahlo wanted to leave immediately, but Rivera talked her out of it, convincing her that she had to stay until after the show to make sure that her paintings were sent safely home.

Breton's "Mexique" exhibit finally opened on March 10. With the threat of war on the horizon, there were very few sales. Kahlo hated the layout of the show. Her paintings were surrounded by arts and crafts and photographs from Mexico—"junk," as she called it. Kahlo spoke very little French, so only a few people bothered to talk to her. Deciding that she had had enough of Europe, Kahlo canceled her scheduled show in London. Certainly, her decision was made partly out of loneliness and homesickness.

Fortunately, there were favorable reviews. Best of all, the most prestigious museum in Europe, the Louvre, purchased Kahlo's painting *The Frame*. Rivera boasted about the sale to everyone he knew—

none of the Mexican muralists had ever been invited
to have their work hung in the Louvre.

Kahlo left Paris on March 25, 1939. Her first stop
was not Mexico but New York. She was hoping to
revive her romance with Nickolas Muray, but she was
disappointed. The photographer had fallen in love
with another woman and did not want to continue
the affair. He married in June.

Things were even worse in Mexico. Rivera's ha-
tred for the Mexican Communist party had caused
him to support a presidential candidate far to the right
of a man favored by both the Communists and Trotsky.
Trotsky and Rivera quarreled bitterly, and by the time
Kahlo arrived in Mexico, Rivera had asked Trotsky to
vacate the Blue House, even refusing Trotsky's offer of
rent. Supporters collected funds to buy the Trotskys
their own home, also in Coyoacán. The guards and
alarm systems were transferred to the new house.
When Trotsky and Natalia Sedova moved, Trotsky left
Frida's self-portrait behind.

A month later, Rivera and Kahlo separated, and
Kahlo moved into the Blue House. The couple filed
for divorce in the fall. Rumors abounded about the
reasons for the sudden split. Some thought it was
because Kahlo had told Rivera that she was in love
with Muray. Others linked Rivera with Hollywood
movie star Paulette Goddard, who had moved into the
San Angel Inn across from Rivera's home and had
posed for him. Neither Rivera nor Kahlo answered
questions about the split. Rivera joked and said that
his biographer considered the relationship permanent,
and he wanted to prove him wrong. He had "magnifi-
cent relations" with Kahlo, he insisted, and added that
the breakup would help Kahlo's blossoming career.
Kahlo wrote to Nickolas Muray: "There is nobody in
the world who has suffered as much as I do."

As in other periods of unhappiness, Kahlo's physical ailments intensified. But this time she took comfort in her art. When she was confined to her bed, Kahlo used the old method that her mother had improvised so many years ago—a mirror and an easel suspended from the canopy above her. Once again cutting her hair short, she painted *Self-Portrait with Cropped Hair*. In this painting, an almost expressionless Kahlo sits in a chair, dressed in an oversized man's suit. She holds a pair of scissors, and her shorn hair covers her leg, the chair, and the floor around her. At the top of the painting, there is a musical notation and two lines of a song: "You know that if I loved you, it was for your hair, / Now that you're shorn, I love you no more."

Rivera often told friends that Kahlo produced her best work during their two-year separation. Kahlo had a different memory of that time. She was so depressed she even considered suicide. Filled with blood and skeletons, her paintings displayed her unhealthy preoccupation with death. Religious symbols crept into her work as well. In one self-portrait, a calm-looking Kahlo wore a crown of thorns. "Let me tell you kid," she wrote to Muray, "this time has been the worst in my whole life."

THE TWO FRIDAS

On January 9, 1940, the day her divorce was finalized, Kahlo completed her first large canvas, *The Two Fridas.* In the double portrait, as Kahlo called it, the two Fridas sit on a bench, holding hands. One wears a lacy Victorian gown; the other, a Tehuana outfit. Both of their hearts are exposed and linked by a long artery. The more feminine Frida's heart is injured, and blood drips onto her elegant white dress. The other Frida's heart is intact, and she clasps a tiny portrait of Diego Rivera. *The Two Fridas* was an obvious message to Rivera: Kahlo was two women, one weak and vulnerable, the other a survivor.

The Two Fridas, along with another large canvas, *The Wounded Table,* was shown at the International Exhibition of Surrealism, which opened on January 17, 1940, in Mexico City. Kahlo's popularity soared among the surrealists, but it was still difficult to sell her paintings, even though Rivera sent potential buyers to the Blue House to view her work. When Kahlo did make a sale, paintings that would later be worth hundreds of thousands of dollars went for a few hundred. A major reason was her unwillingness to paint in a style more acceptable to the general public.

At this point, there really did appear to be two Frida Kahlos.

Kahlo and Rivera enjoy a quiet moment on a stairway at the Blue House during the mid-1940s. After the couple's remarriage in 1940, Rivera had moved into the Blue House; though his philandering continued to torment Kahlo, his presence in her life was essential to her health and her work.

99

One lived in the Blue House in Coyoacán, lonely and miserable. She drank heavily to dull her excruciating back pain. Ordered to have complete bed rest, she spent long periods encased in a torturous boxlike device that was designed to immobilize her spine. This Frida Kahlo seemed to prefer solitude, especially discouraging visitors who were also friends of Rivera. Instead of people, she surrounded herself with a menagerie—monkeys, dogs, parrots, and even a frog.

The second Frida Kahlo was often seen with a cluster of people, arriving with great fanfare at concerts at the National Palace. Rivera would often be the only man in the crowd, flanked by his two daughters, a startling combination of ex-lovers and ex-wives, and perhaps his latest flame. A laughing and carefree Kahlo would be in the midst of the entourage, wearing her most colorful outfits and dripping with jewelry.

Observers of Mexico City's social scene delighted in these public displays; before long, though, Kahlo and Rivera were connected with far less frivolous events. In May 1940, a group of Stalinists, led by Rivera's fellow muralist David Siqueiros, staged a military-style raid on Leon Trotsky's home, hurling firebombs and raking the house with machine-gun fire. The Trotskys barely escaped with their lives. Because of his public dispute with the exiled revolutionary, Rivera was a potential suspect in the assassination plot; in order to avoid police questioning, he left for San Francisco with his favorite model of the moment. (Siqueiros was eventually convicted but spent less than a year in prison.) Finally, on August 20, Stalin obtained his goal when Ramón Mercador, a self-styled student who had infiltrated Trotsky's household, snuck up behind the Old Man and struck him in the head with a mountain climber's ice ax. Trotsky died in the hospital on the following day.

Because Kahlo had known Mercador in Paris and befriended him when he came to Mexico, she and her sister Cristina were dragged off to police headquarters, held for two days, and subjected to many hours of interrogation. Kahlo called Rivera, informing him that the police had ransacked the San Angel house in search of evidence and that her doctors had recommended drastic spinal surgery. She had visions of her own death.

Worried about Kahlo's physical and emotional condition, Rivera consulted with Dr. Eloesser. Believing that Kahlo often fell ill and underwent unnecessary surgery when she felt rejected by Rivera, Eloesser insisted that Kahlo come to San Francisco so that he could personally examine her. He also appealed to Rivera to remarry Kahlo in order to help restore her health.

Kahlo arrived in San Francisco in September. After Eloesser examined her, he declared that surgery was uncalled for. He prescribed bed rest, told Kahlo to stay away from alcohol, and put her on a proper diet. Rivera went through with his part of the plan. On December 8, 1940, he and Kahlo were married by a municipal judge in an almost secret ceremony. There were no photographers, no reception, not even a celebratory party. Rivera returned immediately to work. Two weeks later, Kahlo left for home to spend Christmas with her family.

By February, with Trotsky's assassin in custody and Rivera's work in San Francisco completed, the painter returned to Mexico. This time he went to live at the Blue House, where Kahlo had redecorated and prepared a special bedroom for him. He continued to use the San Angel home for his studio and his many trysts with visiting tourists and other female admirers.

The next few years were apparently the most tranquil of Kahlo's life. However, this was not one of her lazy periods, despite the gradual decline of her health. She took care of Rivera's business affairs and her own, supervised the couple's three servants, visited her family and friends, and entertained. She would often slip out to Garibaldi Square to hear the mariachi bands. When Rivera and his assistant, Emmy Lou Packard, attended classical concerts, Kahlo, her old sense of humor reviving, sometimes dressed Packard up in her own native costumes.

Kahlo's health took a turn for the worse after her father died in the spring of 1941, but by the following year she and Rivera began construction in southern Mexico City on a complex project they named Ana-huacalli. Rivera envisioned the huge spread as a ranch with animals, a museum for his vast collection of pre-Columbian statuary, as well as a studio. Kahlo had bought the land, planning to house Spanish refugees there. Kahlo and Rivera put every extra penny they had into the project, but by 1943, they no longer had the resources to finish the job.

In Mexico, the attitude toward the left became more positive during World War II, when the Soviet Union joined Great Britain and the United States to fight against Germany, Japan, and Italy—the Axis Powers. Rivera was granted membership in the Cole-

Kahlo's studio in the Blue House, with The Last Embrace, *one of her most magical paintings, on the easel. The brightness and order of the room reflect the relative tranquillity of Kahlo's life during the 1940s, when she produced many of her finest works.*

gio Nacional and given a teaching post at the National School of Painting and Sculpture, called La Esmeralda by its students after the street where it was located. Talented students from poor families studied at the school without paying tuition. In 1943, Kahlo taught beginners' classes at La Esmeralda too.

It was the kind of assignment that Kahlo liked best. She had always enjoyed being around young people, and she hated to see talent go to waste. She instructed her pupils to paint freely. Instead of using the traditional method of having them copy lifeless objects arranged on a table, she told them to paint the things they knew best. Realizing that prejudice against darker-skinned people had motivated many young Mexicans to imitate the culture of the United States, Kahlo encouraged her pupils to take pride in their Mexican roots. Almost always wearing some kind of medical contraption or even walking on crutches, she took them to working-class bars to drink and to eat local dishes, sang Mexican folk songs to them, and took them to marketplaces, factories, and political demonstrations.

It was one of the most fulfilling assignments of Kahlo's life, but the long journey into the city became more and more difficult. She offered to continue the classes in her garden. At first all of her pupils came, but soon only four stalwarts remained: three young men—Arturo García Bustos, Guillermo Monroy, Arturo Estrada—and one young woman, Fanny Rabel. They became deeply devoted to Kahlo, proudly calling themselves Los Fridos.

Not satisfied to simply instruct the young artists, Kahlo looked for ways to advance their careers. In 1943, government permission was granted for Los Fridos to paint a mural on the wall of La Rosita, a typical bar in a working-class neighborhood near Coyoacán. When the walls were completed in the middle of June, there was a lively street fiesta. The young artists were quickly offered other commissions. They were especially delighted at the chance to decorate a drab government-built complex where poor laundresses toiled, washing the clothes of the wealthy.

After 1945, when Los Fridos graduated from La Esmeralda, Kahlo continued to help them find jobs in the art world and exhibit their works. In later years, the four Fridos talked often about the love they had felt for their teacher and friend. Even when she was trapped in one of her many casts, they remembered, Kahlo had joked about it, encouraging them to help her decorate it with paints and decals.

Despite the brave front Kahlo put on for Los Fridos and other friends, by 1945 her suffering had increased almost beyond endurance. She got through her days by using massive doses of painkillers and nipping at her ever-present flask of tequila or brandy. Perhaps realizing that her remaining time would be short, Kahlo started a diary, filling the pages with scattered notes and sketches. In her letters to friends over the years, she had often written, "Do not forget me." Now she sent her photograph to dozens of people—former Cachuchas, political allies, old loves, and fellow artists.

Rivera undoubtedly noticed Kahlo's rapid deterioration, but it did little to change his behavior. Government mural commissions were pouring in again, and he absented himself for long hours while painting at several sites. Left alone most of the time and finding it more and more difficult to get around, Kahlo concentrated on her own work.

In 1945, she spent three months laboring to finish a privately commissioned work, *Moses,* which turned out to be one of her most complex creations. The birth of Moses was at the center of the canvas, but the rest of the space was filled with miniature portraits of many heroes and villains, ranging from the heroes of

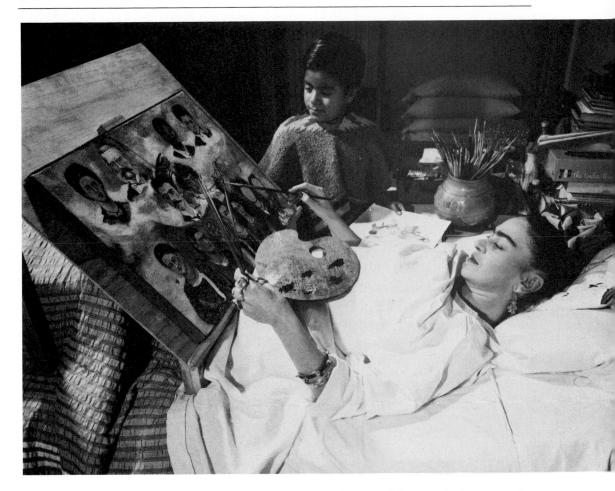

Recovering form serious spinal surgery in 1950, Kahlo paints in her bed in Mexico City's English Hospital while a young assistant looks on. Always interested in young people, Kahlo had taught at the National School of Painting and Sculpture until her physical ailments made it impossible for her to get around.

socialism to Adolf Hitler, Buddha, and Aztec gods. *Moses* was included in the annual National Exhibition at Mexico City's Palace of Fine Arts. In September 1946, recovering from a major spinal operation and stumbling from the weight of yet another plaster cast, Kahlo smilingly accepted one of the few prizes given out at the exhibition.

During the most recent surgery, a piece of Kahlo's pelvic bone had been fused to her vertebrae, and a long metal rod had been inserted to stabilize her spine. After weeks of severe pain, her health and spirits improved dramatically, and she turned with new vigor to her painting. Before long, though, the terrible pain returned. Kahlo's physicians discovered that she had developed a serious bone disease—osteomyelitis. Once again she was entrapped in a corset, this one made of steel.

Kahlo now seemed to be pouring her physical pain out onto her canvases. In *The Little Deer,* Kahlo's own head, crowned by a pair of antlers, appears on the arrow-pierced body of a young stag. In *Tree of Hope,* another double portrait, a tearful Kahlo stands guard over her double, who is stretched out on a hospital gurney with two deep gashes in her exposed back. Kahlo sent *The Little Deer* to her New York friends Arcady and Lina Boytler, accompanying the gift with a poem. Along with expressions of her sadness and her affection for the Boytlers, the poem includes a wistful note of optimism: "When the deer returns / strong, happy and cured / the wounds he has now / will all be erased."

Some of Kahlo's wounds continued to be inflicted by Rivera. In late 1948, he became involved with another of his models. This time, Kahlo perceived a genuine threat because the model was Mexico's most celebrated and glamorous actress, María Felix. The newspapers reported that Rivera planned to divorce Kahlo and marry the sultry love goddess. Rivera denied any involvement with Felix, but he admitted that he intended to divorce Kahlo because he was "bad for her health." Kahlo claimed to be amused by the gossip, but she moved out of the Blue House and rented an apartment in Mexico City.

Rivera is prominently featured in Kahlo's weeping self-portraits of 1948 and 1949. In *Diego and I,* his face appears in the middle of Kahlo's forehead. *The Last Embrace of the Universe, the Earth (Mexico), Diego, Me, and Señor Xolotl,* one of her most magical paintings, depicts Kahlo in the embrace of a gigantic earth goddess, while she herself cradles in her arms the nude, childlike form of Rivera.

By late 1949, it was apparent that Kahlo was not going to recover. She wrote a detailed letter to Dr. Eloesser, describing the various opinions of her Mexican doctors. One wanted to amputate her right foot; another recommended injections of various gases; a third recommended a new spinal fusion. "They are driving me crazy and making me desperate. What should I do?" she pleaded.

Eloesser came to Mexico City and examined Kahlo in early January 1950. He agreed with the spinal fusion option, and Dr. Juan Farill, whom Kahlo liked because he himself was lame, performed the surgery on January 26. Kahlo spent almost a year recovering in Mexico City's English Hospital. Rivera took a room next to hers and spent many nights at the hospital.

To some observers, there were two very different patients called Frida Kahlo. One held parties in her room almost every night, roaring at Laurel and Hardy and Charlie Chaplin movies, eating Mexican specialties with gusto. This Kahlo wore flowers in her hair and joked with visitors. She decorated her room with sugar skulls (a traditional Mexican treat) and a Soviet flag. Many mornings she painted in her bed, working on *My Family*, a pictorial family tree that included her parents and grandparents: her older sisters are shown as sour, middle-aged women, but Frida and Cristina are young and beautiful. Guillermo Kahlo looks the way he had when Kahlo was a little girl.

The second Frida Kahlo fretted when Rivera was gone. She looked pale, aging, and filled with fear. She found it unbearable to be alone and depended completely on her injections of Demerol.

Kahlo returned to the Blue House on time for the Christmas holidays in December 1950. She sat in a wheelchair and participated in a carefree celebration of her second marriage to Rivera. Unable to walk much, she moved her bedroom next to her upstairs studio and spent much of her time alone, painting between her Demerol injections and glasses of tequila. From time to time, close friends visited her, and she could always count on her sister Cristina's daily visit.

After another operation to remove an infected bone graft, Kahlo began to talk less about her disintegrating body and more about her art. She had been allowed to rejoin the Communist party, and possibly to make amends for her fling with Trotsky and Trotskyism, she published an article in a Mexican newspaper, *Excelsior,* heaping abuse on her dead friend and former lover. She called Trotsky cowardly and pretentious and claimed that he had robbed her home. She had never wanted him to come to Mexico, she declared, but Rivera's "sense of hospitality" had won the day.

As alcohol and drugs became the central focus of her life, Kahlo's work suffered. Her paintings lost their

Kahlo is flanked by three of the four art students who called themselves los Fridos: left to right, Fanny Rabel, Arturo Estrada, and Arturo García Bustos. In addition to helping her students develop their talent, Kahlo taught them to understand and cherish their Mexican heritage.

vibrancy, and her usual meticulousness disappeared. She made several suicide attempts, disguised by her protective family and friends as accidental drug overdoses. Cristina Kahlo came to stay at the Blue House, making sure that there was always someone watching her sister when one of the round-the-clock nurses stepped out of the room. On a few occasions, Kahlo insisted on going out for a brief trip to a nearby town or to dinner, but more and more she was confined to bed. One of her few happy moments, at the end of 1952, was a joyous street fiesta to celebrate the repainting of the faded mural on the wall of La Rosita. A few days later, Kahlo was brought downstairs to join in a celebration of Rivera's 66th birthday and the anniversary of their second marriage.

Kahlo wanted Rivera near her night and day and complained bitterly about his absences. As she grew more dependent, he became almost frenetically busier, attempting a new experimental underwater mural at the Lerma waterworks, and—as part of his effort to achieve readmission to the Communist party—joining with David Siqueiros in an effort to organize an international meeting to protest the spread of nuclear weapons.

A retrospective of Kahlo's paintings was being planned at the National Institute of Fine Arts, but the word spread that Kahlo might not live to see her first solo show in Mexico. A gallery in Mexico City's affluent Pink Zone offered to house the show and mount it quickly. Kahlo personally designed invitations and sent them out to hundreds of people.

Her doctors advised Kahlo against attending, but she refused to miss the event. On April 13, 1953, her huge four-poster bed, complete with its canopy, mirror, signed photographs, and other decorations, was brought to the gallery and placed in the center of the room. Her paintings hung on the walls around it.

As a crowd gathered, an ambulance and motorcy-
cle escorts approached the gallery, sirens blaring.
Kahlo, heavily drugged but dressed in all her finery,
was brought in on a stretcher. Looking more dead
than alive, Kahlo stretched out on her bed in the
middle of her paintings, regaling the spectators with
stories, songs, and jokes. Everyone filed past the bed
and received a personal greeting. Novices and critics
alike were awed by the paintings, whose impact was
even greater when viewed in a major collection.
Kahlo was no longer "Little Frida" but an artist of
immense stature.

In August 1953, just four months after the show,
Kahlo was back in the hospital, shouting in protest
when the doctors told her that her right leg had
developed gangrene and would have to be amputated.
Her psychiatrist and her closest friends persuaded her
that the surgery was necessary to save her life. Her old
Cachucha girlfriend, Adelina Zendejas, reminded
Kahlo of the many times she had referred to herself as
a gimp with a pegleg. This time, Zendejas told her, she
could learn to walk on an artificial leg, a real pegleg,
and she would be free of pain. But Rivera had no
illusions about the outcome. "This is going to kill
her," he tearfully declared.

After the amputation, Kahlo joked with visitors,
but those close to her knew that her spirit had been
broken. When she returned home she would not talk
to anyone, had no interest in painting, and refused to
use her artificial leg. Then, in the spring of 1954, her
second persona seemed to briefly emerge. She had
special red boots designed with bells attached to them,
and she invited people to come and look at her stump.
Kahlo asked to have her bed moved to the hallway,
where she could have a view of the gardens. Relying
on drugs to conquer her pain, she either painted in
her bed or used a wheelchair to reach her studio.

Rivera, unable to face Kahlo's obvious decline, fell into his customary behavior, staying away from the house for days at a time. Whenever he failed to come home, Kahlo abused her sisters and the servants, demanding more drugs. She refused to have children in the house, resenting their health and youth. On two occasions, she was taken to the hospital for unexplained reasons. It was whispered that she had tried to commit suicide again. On each occasion, Rivera suddenly reappeared, only to be driven away again by the intensity of Kahlo's suffering.

On July 2, 1954, 10,000 demonstrators gathered in Mexico City in a chilling downpour to protest U.S. military intervention in Guatemala, where a democratically elected government had made reforms that threatened U.S. business interests. As the long march began, the press caught sight of Diego Rivera pushing a wheelchair. In it was Frida Kahlo, bundled up, without makeup, her head covered by a wrinkled scarf. She had been racked with bronchial pneumonia for weeks, but she refused to miss the demonstration. In one hand she held a placard with a peace dove stenciled on it. Her other hand was raised in a clenched fist as she yelled with the others, "¡Gringos asesinos, fuera!"—"Yanqui assassins, get out!"

In a few hours, she was back at home, raging with fever. Four days later, she celebrated her 47th birthday, appearing downstairs in a white dress to greet more than 100 guests. On July 12, she presented Rivera with an anniversary gift, a ring, and retired for the night. He returned to San Angel and was awakened with the news that Kahlo had been found dead at dawn.

Lupe Marín and Rivera's art dealer, Emma Hurtado, helped Kahlo's nurse dress the dead artist and adorn her with jewelry, the way she always liked to look in public. Her body was brought to the Palace of

Fine Arts, where hundreds came to pay their last respects. Her family, friends, and several government dignitaries, including ex-president Cárdenas, marched in the funeral procession. Rivera had promised that there would be no political demonstrations, but at one point, one of her loyal Fridos, Arturo García Bustos, created an uproar by flipping the flowers off the coffin and covering it instead with a red flag, the symbol of the Communist party.

Kahlo had asked to be cremated. With her usual black humor she had said that after all the corsets she had had to wear, she could not bear the thought of being stuffed into a coffin. Like her art exhibition the previous year, the cremation seemed almost a surrealist event. As an automatic cart carried Kahlo's body toward the oven, hundreds of people sang the Mexican national anthem, the Communist *Internationale,* and some of Kahlo's favorite Mexican folk songs. As Kahlo's body entered the oven, the intense heat caused it to rise up in a sitting position, her hair forming a ring of fire around her face. Cristina Kahlo screamed as her sister disappeared into the flames.

A few hours later, Rivera took Kahlo's ashes to the Blue House, where she had been born and spent most of her life. In July 1956, a year and a half before his own death, he donated the house to the Mexican people and reopened it as the Frida Kahlo Museum. One of Kahlo's last paintings occupied a prominent place in the museum's first exhibition: a still life of watermelons, some cut and some whole, with the inscription "Viva la Vida" (Long Live Life).

By the 1970s, when Frida Kahlo had been dead for almost two decades, feminists in the United States and Europe elevated her into something close to an idol, focusing on her struggle to be recognized as an artist, her frustrated desire for motherhood, and her difficulties with a philandering husband. In the 1990s,

Diego Rivera and a host of friends and admirers surround Kahlo's coffin during her funeral on July 14, 1954. Andrés Iduarte, director of the National Institute of Fine Arts, concluded his funeral oration with this tribute: "Friend, sister of the people, great daughter of Mexico: you are still alive."

Kahlo became internationally celebrated, numbering among her fans and collectors such pop culture figures as the singer Madonna.

Whether Kahlo truly deserves to be considered a feminist role model will be the subject of intense discussion for years to come. Critics and scholars will also argue about the proper category for her art, which includes elements of surrealism, naturalism, and other techniques. There is little debate, however, about the artistic power and emotional impact of Kahlo's paintings. Hayden Herrera, Kahlo's principal biographer in English, has written that "for all her anguish, Frida Kahlo's final gift is the preeminence of joy." She will continue to be admired and honored by those who love art, not merely as an exceptional woman artist or Mexican artist but as one of the truly great painters of the 20th century.

CHRONOLOGY

1907	Born Magdalena Carmen Frieda Kahlo y Calderón in Coyoacán, Mexico, on July 6
1913	Afflicted with poliomyelitis at age six; her right leg is left permanently withered
1922	Enters National Preparatory School in Mexico City; becomes member of the Cachuchas and first meets Diego Rivera
1925	Severely injured in bus accident on September 17
1926	While recovering from her injuries, paints first portraits of herself and friends
1927	Participates in political activities at University of Mexico and joins Young Communist League
1928	Becomes reacquainted with Rivera; their romance begins
1929	Kahlo marries Rivera on August 21; resigns from Communist party when Rivera is expelled
1930	Travels to San Francisco with Rivera; meets Dr. Leo Eloesser; paints *Luther Burbank,* the first work in her distinctive style
1932	Lives in Detroit with Rivera; suffers a miscarriage; paints *Henry Ford Hospital;* returns to Mexico when her mother dies
1933	Travels to New York with Rivera; his Rockefeller Center mural causes controversy; Kahlo expresses her longing for Mexico in paintings such as *My Dress Hangs There*

1934	Kahlo and Rivera build twin homes in San Angel; Rivera becomes romantically involved with Kahlo's sister Cristina
1937	Exiled Soviet revolutionary Leon Trotsky and his wife arrive in Mexico; Kahlo has love affair with Trotsky, who encourages her to paint
1938	Kahlo's paintings exhibited at University of Mexico and in her first solo exhibit at Julien Levy Gallery in New York
1939	Kahlo participates in surrealist exhibit in Paris; the Louvre Museum buys her painting *The Frame;* Kahlo helps refugees from Fascist Spain get to Mexico; Kahlo and Rivera divorce
1940	*The Two Fridas* and *The Wounded Table* are exhibited in International Surrealism Exhibition in Mexico City; Leon Trotsky is assassinated; Kahlo and Rivera remarry in San Francisco on December 8
1941	Kahlo and Rivera move into the Blue House in Coyoacán; Kahlo's father dies
1943	Kahlo exhibits her work in several important group shows and begins teaching at the National School of Painting and Sculpture
1944–49	In declining health, paints *The Broken Column, Tree of Hope, The Little Deer,* and other major works
1950	Hospitalized for a year in Mexico City after another spinal operation; is readmitted to Communist party
1953	Attends her first solo show in Mexico; undergoes amputation of right leg on July 27
1954	Dies on July 13 at the Blue House
1958	Blue House is opened to the public as the Frida Kahlo Museum

FURTHER READING

Cockcroft, James D. *Mexico.* Rev. ed. New York: Monthly Review Press, 1990.

———. *Diego Rivera.* New York: Chelsea House, 1991.

Drucker, Malka. *Frida Kahlo: Torment and Triumph in Her Life and Art.* New York: Bantam, 1991.

Garza, Hedda. *Leon Trotsky.* New York: Chelsea House, 1986.

Herrera, Hayden. *Frida: A Biography of Frida Kahlo.* New York: HarperCollins, 1983.

———. *Frida Kahlo: The Paintings.* New York: HarperCollins, 1991.

Rivera, Diego, with Gladys March. *My Art, My Life: An Autobiography.* New York: Citadel, 1960.

Wolfe, Bertram D. *The Fabulous Life of Diego Rivera.* New York: Stein and Day, 1963.

Zamora, Martha. *Frida Kahlo: The Brush of Anguish.* San Francisco: Chronicle Books, 1990.

INDEX

HEDDA GARZA lives in upstate New York, where she works as a freelance writer and lecturer. Her articles on hidden Mexican and U.S. history have appeared in many national magazines and newspapers, and her *Watergate Investigation Index* won the Best Academic Book Award from *Choice* magazine. She is also the author of *Joan Baez* and *Pablo Casals* in the Chelsea House HISPANICS OF ACHIEVEMENT series, as well as four biographies in the Chelsea House series WORLD LEADERS—PAST & PRESENT.

RODOLFO CARDONA is professor of Spanish and comparative literature at Boston University. A renowned scholar, he has written many works of criticism, including *Ramón, a Study of Gómez de la Serna and His Works and Visión del esperpento: Teoría y práctica del esperpento en Valle-Inclán*. Born in San José, Costa Rica, he earned his B.A. and M.A. from Louisiana State University and received a Ph.D. from the University of Washington. He has taught at Case Western Reserve University, the University of Pittsburgh, the University of Texas at Austin, the University of New Mexico, and Harvard University.

JAMES COCKCROFT is currently a visiting professor of Latin American and Caribbean studies at the State University of New York at Albany. A three-time Fulbright scholar, he earned a Ph.D. from Stanford University and has taught at the University of Massachusetts, the University of Vermont, and the University of Connecticut. He is the author or coauthor of numerous books on Latin American subjects, including *Neighbors in Turmoil: Latin America, The Hispanic Experience in the United States: Contemporary Issues and Perspectives,* and *Outlaws in the Promised Land: Mexican Immigrant Workers and America's Future.*